Sullied Magnificence:

The Theatre of Mark O'Rowe

Sullied Magnificence:

The Theatre of Mark O'Rowe

edited by Sara Keating and Emma Creedon

Carysfort Press

A Carysfort Press Book in association with Peter Lang
Sullied Magnificence: The Theatre of Mark O'Rowe
Edited by Sara Keating and Emma Creedon
First published in Ireland in 2015 as a paperback original by
Carysfort Press,
58 Woodfield, Scholarstown Road
Dublin 16, Ireland

ISBN 978-1-78874-783-7
©2015 Copyright remains with the authors
Typeset by Carysfort Press

Cover design by eprint limited

This book is published with the financial assistance of
The Arts Council (An Chomhairle Ealaíon) Dublin, Ireland

Caution: All rights reserved. No part of this book may be printed or reproduced or utilized in any form or by any electronic, mechanical, or other means, now known or hereafter invented including photocopying and recording, or in any information storage or retrieval system without permission in writing from the publishers.

Table of Contents

Acknowledgements — ix

Introduction — 1
   Sara Keating and Emma Creedon

1 | A Sense of Place, A Place of Dread — 7
   Jimmy Fay

2 | 'Keep the Aspidistra Flying': The Satirizing of Celtic Tiger, 'Aspirational' Lifestyles in Mark O'Rowe's Early Work — 13
   David S. Clare

3 | Expletive Narrative: Mark O'Rowe's *Howie the Rookie*: The Early Critical Reception of Dublin's Dark Diegetic Narrative — 27
   Thomas B. Costello

4 | The Small Guy with the Glasses. — 41
   Aidan Kelly

5 | *Crestfall*: A Production Study. — 49
   Sara Keating

6 | Performativity and Class in Mark O'Rowe's Monologue Plays. — 63
   Tim Barrett

7 | From 'Up-Yer-Hole' Theatre to the Shakesqueer: 79
    Made in China (2001) and
    Henry IV Part I (2002)
    Emma Creedon

8 | At the Terminus in the Brain: Illusions of Consciousness
    in Mark O'Rowe's *Terminus*. 91
    Marie Kelly

9 | Interwoven Locality and a Globalized Dublin: Mark
    O'Rowe's *Terminus*. 105
    Nelson Barre

10 | Violated Sanctuaries: The Screenplays of Mark O'Rowe 122
    Harvey O'Brien

11 | Review of *Our Few and Evil Days* 137
    Emilie Pine

12 | A Tallaght of the Mind: In Conversation with 141
    Mark O'Rowe
    Cormac O'Brien

Performances and Bibliography 155

Biographies 159

Index 163

Acknowledgements

The editors would like to thank all the contributors, in particular Jimmy Fay, Garry Hynes, Aidan Kelly, Frances O'Connor, Aisling O'Sullivan, and Eileen Walsh, for sharing their experience of producing the work of Mark O'Rowe for the stage; Fintan O'Toole, for permission to reproduce his original review of *Crestfall* and a generous endorsement; Pat Redmond for providing a stunning cover image; The Abbey Theatre Archive; The Gate Theatre, for access to their archive and permission to reproduce programme material from *Crestfall*; Professor Anthony Roche; commissioning editor, Dr Eamonn Jordan for encouragement and advice; Rachel Andrews, for kind permission to reprint her reviews of *Crestfall*; and Mark O'Rowe, for providing access to unpublished material, an in depth interview, and, of course, his brilliant plays.

Introduction

Sara Keating and Emma Creedon

In his 2007 play *Terminus*, Mark O'Rowe brings the audience on a whirlwind journey though Dublin city, from its inner-city core to the outer reaches of the Red Cow Roundabout and beyond. We see familiar landmarks from different perspectives: Ormond Quay from the cab of a stolen lorry; Jervis Street from the precarious height of a crane. But O'Rowe brings us on a metaphysical journey too: from purgatorial depravation to ecstatic sexual escape; from the physical space of the theatre into the limitless depths of our imaginations. Scanning the city from the heights of a ride she catches with a demon, the character of A evokes the 'sullied magnificence' of the city below her, its majestic resonances and compromised beauty (*Terminus*, 11). It is, more than anything, this blend of base subject and artistic poetry that defines the work of Mark O'Rowe, whose first play was produced 20 years ago this year.

Terminus typifies the bold experiment and challenge of an O'Rowe play. A series of three overlapping monologues, it is dense with imagery and linguistic experiment. If the subject matter is drawn from a kind of comic-book fantasy, its heightened poetry and complex rhyming patterns sculpt high art from some of the most sordid impulses of human behaviour. Consider his 2003 play for women, *Crestfall*, where rape, abortion and bestiality feature significantly in the exploration of female sexuality. Or his most recent play, *Our Few and Evil Days* (2014), where a family is torn apart by a son's incestuous impulses.

O'Rowe is best known for using first-person address to engage sympathy for characters that might easily be considered vile and violent. The dual anti-heroes of *Howie the Rookie* (1999) seem more vulnerable than dangerous when we see the world from their perspective. The character of C in *Terminus* exudes charm as well as menace; as he narrates his journey we see a sensitive soul as well as a serial killer. O'Rowe's characters are heroes in their own worlds, with their own ethical codes and journeys of revenge and honour. As hit-man Drongo in one of O'Rowe's first plays says, right before he raises a gun to shoot a debtor, 'Without moral values, ethics, etiquette, principles, we are without rules ... If I don't stick to my rules, then what am I?' *(The Aspidistra Code: Plays: One,* 40) The criminal character of Lehiff from O'Rowe's 2003 film *Intermission* expresses the complexity of this moral compass with his catchphrase 'be good.'

Although O'Rowe has often been criticized for using what detractors have called a non-dramatic or easy-wipe form, O'Rowe has also experimented with more traditional forms of dramatic realism. *The Aspidistra Code* and *From Both Hips* (1997) are both one-act kitchen-sink dramas, though they feature embryonic reflections of the work to come. Although conventional in form, their extreme characters and revenge plots exploded the realist frame from within. The mid-career play *Made in China* (2001) followed suit, while *Our Few and Evil Days*, playing at the Abbey Theatre as this book was being edited in a production directed by O'Rowe himself, plays with an extreme mode of naturalism.

O'Rowe does not have a preference for one form over another: it is merely a case of how a story can best be told. There is deep metaphorical resonance to his use of the monologue too. His characters are outsiders, alienated from family, friends, and often society at large. On a political level, the monologue is their opportunity to have their voices heard; on a metaphysical level it provides the 'illusion of presence through voices' (*Terminus,* 9), as the character of B puts it; the comfort of words spoken in the dark. And yet O'Rowe's attraction to the monologue seems significant: there is no fourth wall for the audience to hide behind. The monologue has allowed him to break down the barrier between stage and stalls, and 'make the audience complicit.' (Sara Keating, *Mark O'Rowe: The Power to Shock – And Feel, The Irish Times,* 26th September 2014).

This complicity has not been without controversy. The sexual violence of *Crestfall*, divided critics and audiences alike, as did *Terminus*, which features, among other things, a young woman copulating with a demon. On the larger dramatic canvas of *Our Few and Evil Days,* meanwhile, O'Rowe's decision to make visible the dead perpetrator of incest in the play's final moments drew audible inhalations from the audience on the several occasions that the editors of this collection saw it.

This collection balances academic appraisals of O'Rowe's plays and films with personal testimonies from leading Irish theatre practitioners who have been instrumental in ensuring the writer's continued success. Director Jimmy Fay's opening essay recalls how he first encountered O'Rowe when they were in their twenties, both emerging from the 'brutal landscape' that was the Dublin suburb of Tallaght in the 1970s. Fay reflects on the production of *Anna's Ankle* as part of his Theatre of Cruelty Season at the Project Arts Centre in 1997 and the ensuing furore in response to the play's graphic content. This essay traces their subsequent collaboration from their partnership on *Henry IV Part I* at the Peacock Theatre in 2002 to Fay's direction of *Howie the Rookie* in 2006, with an anecdotal and witty pertinence. Actor Aidan Kelly's essay is an equally astute insight into his artistic relationship with O'Rowe, in particular his experience preparing for the role of The Howie Lee for the London premiere of *Howie the Rookie*. Approached by the writer (the 'small guy with the glasses' of the essay's title) in The Sackville Lounge in Dublin in 1998, Kelly agreed to co-star in the play at The Bush Theatre the following year. His essay thoroughly reflects on the actorial challenges posited by the play, notably its monologue form and the difficulties in pitching the Dublin vernacular for a British audience. Thomas B. Costello's essay suitably proposes a complementary analysis of this play in terms of the dramaturgical challenges that the monologue form presents. His essay employs Brian Richardson's writings on diegetic narration and implied authorship to offer an original reading of O'Rowe's distinctive narrative style. Tim Barrett also concentrates on the formal qualities of the dramatic writing, starting with O'Rowe's lesser-known and as of yet unpublished *Anna's Ankle* and uncovering how issues of performativity and class equally apply to *Howie the Rookie*, *Crestfall* and *Terminus*. In particular, Barrett reveals how the 'illocutionary force of the monologues shapes middle-class encounters with represented worlds of brutality and abjection.'

Sara Keating's production study of *Crestfall* offers an interrogatory analysis of a challenging piece of theatre for both the audience and those involved in its production. It includes testimonies by O'Rowe himself, the director Garry Hynes, set designer Francis O'Connor, actors Eileen Walsh and Aisling O'Sullivan, as well as subsequent reactions to the play in the media. *Crestfall* is a testimony to O'Rowe's ability to push the boundaries of both theatrical and moral acceptability and Keating's case study attests to its relevance and importance within the writer's dramatic canon.

Harvey O'Brien's essay on O'Rowe's writing for film is an essential addition to this collection as it exposes how the writer's authorial presence is equally evident in his original feature screenplays, adaptations, and shorts, as it is in his plays. Moreover, the essays featured in this collection approach O'Rowe's plays with new refreshing theoretical frameworks, accessing the sociological contexts of their conception and offering original readings of O'Rowe's dramatic oeuvre in terms of both Irish and global dramatic trends. David S. Clare's essay focuses on both the writer's early work for theatre and his screenplay for *Intermission* (2003), and demonstrates how these works succeed in satirizing the contemporary society that produced them by mocking the middle-class tendency to procure intercultural, non-Irish identities that usurp their own. On the other hand, Nelson Barre situates *Terminus* (2007) in terms of current definitions of globalization, arguing that critical commentaries on the violence in this play ignore its reliance on 'international interconnectivity.' Barre suggests a prospective redemption for the characters as they strive to transcend the isolated dramatic world of the play. Also in relation to *Terminus*, Marie Kelly probes the Cartesian notion of the *cogito*, demonstrating how the play 'savagely smashes through the Cartesian mirror frame, the illusion upon which the theatre metaphor rests.' Kelly's essay analyses how this shattering of consciousness relates to current discussions on the issue and she contextualizes these arguments in relation to contemporary Irish theatre.

Emma Creedon's essay analyses O'Rowe's *Made in China* (2001) in relation to his adaptation of *Henry IV Part I* for the Peacock stage in 2002. She exposes the thematic similarities between the two plays in terms of 'the legitimacy of ruler-ship, the shackles of inheritance and the cogency of loyalty.' She also notes the formal similarities of the writing in terms of the juxtaposition of 'high' vocabulary, interspersed with 'low' urban slang and how language, like masculinity, becomes performative and a vehicle for supremacy.

In her production review of O'Rowe's most recent play, *Our Few and Evil Days* (2014), Emilie Pine identifies familiar tropes from O'Rowe's earlier work, notably 'men with mother issues, men who do violence (emotional or physical) to women in the name of love [and] women who put up with the violence in the name of love.' However, Pine notes that O'Rowe's dramatization of the 'criminal and merciless side of human nature through grotesque humour and confrontation' jars with the domestic realism of the setting in an unsettling and startling manner. The play, which premiered at the Abbey Theatre in September 2014 as part of the Dublin Theatre Festival, was commissioned by the National Theatre and directed by O'Rowe himself, its production marking the debut appearance of O'Rowe's work on the Abbey main stage.

This collection concludes with a crucial interview with the writer himself, conducted by Cormac O'Brien to coincide with the revival of *Howie the Rookie* at the Project Arts Centre in Dublin in 2013, as performed solely by Tom Vaughan-Lawlor. This interview offers a fascinating insight into O'Rowe's creative processes; it exposes the literary, theatrical and filmic influences on his writing, reflects on the delicate relationship between the spectator and the monologist, and discloses his exciting plans for future projects.

1 | A Sense of Place, A Place of Dread

Jimmy Fay

If you grew up in Tallaght in the 1970s and 1980s and were of a somewhat sensitive nature you learnt to sense trouble like a deer. This didn't mean you always avoided it but to survive any tricky environment you needed to adapt and camouflage. Tallaght was a new town with scarce resources and an ever-growing, young population. It was a brutal landscape.

Like *Salem's Lot* in Stephen King's novel, it was overlooked by 'the house on the hill': The Hellfire Club. In the forests beneath it, the mysterious Lord Massey's ruin lay like a vampire's labyrinthine lair, overgrown by ivy. But the 'town' itself was a vast concrete expanse of inner-city conflict transplanted onto some ill-thought-out 1960s vision of suburbia built on an ancient pagan burial ground. This was the badlands of Tallaght, Támhleacht, its very name evoking its dark history and grim reality: the Gaelic word 'támh' means plague; 'leacht' means grave. Támhleacht was a burial place for people who died of the plague. Tallaght was a place of the dead.

The landscape was a rich combination of mossy woodlands and streams, tamed for a time by the neat, sturdy houses built by the developer McInerney. It was an almost medieval place populated by roaming tribes, maundering wanders and semi-wild animals. From the windows of my classrooms at school, I would watch tramps wander the vast meadows outside and, walking home, see the traveller youths ride their horses through the suburban streets like outlaw cowboys. There was even a lad with a filthy, brown face and vivid blue eyes who seemed to live in an old ruin over the river. His special trick was to leap suddenly out of the bushes, scaring younger kids half to death, before inviting them to ride his 'pet' goat.

The schools were community schools meant to train the artisans of the republic. If you had aspirations you studied hard, worked at your technical drawing and aimed for engineering or, if you were canny, computer programming. Fantasies involved being a rock star or a karate expert. You didn't entertain aristocratic notions of being a poet or involved in theatre.

Although Mark and I grew up a few hundred yards away from each other, we didn't meet until we were in our twenties. We were the same age but a motorway divided our environments. When I did meet him I knew immediately were he'd come from: that, like me, he'd survived 'Tallaghtafornia'.

Gerry Stembridge, who was involved in Dublin Youth Theatre at the time, introduced us and said we should work together: 'sure isn't that what it's all about'. I was running an improvisation workshop for DYT and Mark sat in on it. Afterwards we went for coffee and talked about movies. I liked Mark immediately. He was full of enthusiasms and wit. He knew his pulp and his 'art' and appreciated both equally. He was generous in praise and scathing in his condemnations. But nothing prepared me for reading him. Gerry had already given *The Aspidistra Code* a much acclaimed public reading in the The Peacock in 1997, but I missed it, so I read it in my bedsit where I laughed so loud my neighbours banged on the wall. It was a fantastic noir tale set in the badlands of my youth. I loved it and wanted to direct it. I approached Mark about producing it with Bedrock at the Project Arts Centre but Mark had already moved on, and his second play *From Both Hips* was going into production with Fishamble. He didn't want his first play going on second. To my knowledge *The Aspidistra Code* never did get a professional production here, which is a shame.

A few months later, I met Mark outside a bookshop. I was putting together a season with my company inspired by what was actually a mis-reading of Antonin Artuad's 'Theatre of Cruelty', and I was inviting people outside the core Bedrock members to direct and write and act in it. I told him a little about 'Theatre of Cruelty', and what we were trying to do, but I also said I was thinking of putting Pinter and Beckett into the mix. This excited Mark because, like any emerging writer, he was still discovering his voice and was excited by the elegance and sharp style of those cruel and cool masters. He said he had an idea for something already and within no time he wrote the play and gave me a copy.

Anna's Ankle is one of the darkest, most disturbing, plays I have ever read. I remember being almost scared to turn the page as I went deep into this strange, chilling tale of a film-maker and his pursuit of an ultimate truth: photographing the eyes of Anna as she walks on her stumps after he's cut off her feet. It was unsettling because there was no obvious double meaning, no metaphor of political oppression. It was the pure graphic chill of a misogynist, narcissistic narrator, and it was the first time I ever felt the force of Mark's storytelling. This was not a neat parable wrapped up and ready to be deciphered in some academic way. This was the thing itself: brutal first-person narrative, exquisitely told. Mid-way through, it makes a subtle but key shift from the present to the future tense, but in no way does this ease the growing tension and then horror for the audience. Everybody who read it was either appalled or disgusted by it. I don't remember any defenders.

I told Mark I thought it was really unsettling, and was hesitant to programme it. He said 'what are you doing: a Theatre of Cruelty season or a Theatre of the Mildly Upsetting?' There was no answer to that. I produced *Anna's Ankle* as part of the Fragments series, the first part of Electroshock: A Theatre of Cruelty season in Project @ the Mint in February 1997. It nested there between Samuel Beckett's *Catastrophe* and *What Where?* and Heiner Müller's *Obituary*. It was directed with fierce skill and restraint by John O'Brien, and Patrick Leech gave a brave and spiky performance as the narrator.

And boy, did the audience react! It was like a bomb exploded. They could accept the cruelties of Beckett and Müller and Edward Bond, but the unsettling violence of *Anna's Ankle*, the sheer power of the understated shift from present to imagined storytelling, was too much. They reacted, the way weird and new things are often reacted to, with sneers and condemnation. One night, as one punter was leaving at the end of the play, he shouted out the final lines of the play from the back of the auditorium: 'Too much? (Beat) Too much!" Yes it could do with some cuts alright!' What struck me most was that he had stayed and listened until the very end of the play, before making his protest. The power of the storytelling had held him; the images, although repulsive, were compelling.

This was 'in-yer-face theatre', and the press went all-out in their attack. One evening paper stated it was the most vile, upsetting piece of theatre they ever had the misfortune to witness. You can't buy those kind of reviews and we sold out the season. Fintan O'Toole was the only critic who attempted to contextualize it. This was Mark's first professionally produced piece (I think he got paid something), and

O'Toole knew he'd witnessed a new and disturbing voice enter the Irish theatre landscape.

Mark's next play *Howie the Rookie* was fuelled by the myths and pulp violence that would be recognizable to anyone raised in an under-resourced town with a large, young population. It presented a landscape of concrete, fields and motorways, full of disenchanted youths that were vaguely in love with death. Death was ever-present. It was a snarling black dog on the edge of the estate, or two exotic rumble fish in a tank, one with a stringy poo. It offered an embrace, an escape, an avoidance of reality and its nasty day-glow of bills and butter vouchers, affairs and alcohol. It was a hoody nightmare for the middle-classes, a tale of revenge and kitchen-sink realism poeticized into something as redemptive, cathartic and violent as a revenge saga. It is one of the truly great epic plays of our times, and it floored me when I saw it on opening night at the Bush Theatre in February 1999.

What floored me the most was the language of the play and the joy in the telling, the words weaving in and out of each other: words upon words upon words. Nobody I knew, from anywhere, had ever played with language like this. It wasn't rap and it wasn't poetry. It was more like a whirlwind twisting you up and throwing you about, leaving you to pick up the pieces. Or lose its sense all together. Mark made it seem so simple. I'd heard other playwrights describe their own writing as cinematic but this really was: it was sparse, simple, fragmented, straight-ahead storytelling, using words alone to evoke atmosphere and build tension. The performances by Aidan Kelly and Karl Shiels are etched into the fabric of my mind as part of that merry go round.

Mark and I were firm friends by now and we really wanted to work together; me directing, Mark adapting, and we settled on *Henry IV, Part I*, which was staged at the Peacock in November 2002. (Originally, we were supposed to do *Part II* as well, but the second part got dropped for reasons too confusing to recall.) It was probably not the most obvious project for either of us to embark on, but it had a couple of crucial elements that attracted us both. It is a play about wayward youth and responsibility, hedonism and facing up to reality. We were in our early thirties at this stage, and the stark truth of 'will you ever grow up'? was squaring up to us in the mirror a bit too often. It is also one of Shakespeare's most verbally dexterous rhapsodies, and Mark felt eager and willing to get his knife into it, to transform it into a different beast altogether. He liked the thrill of paring it back to reveal as stark and sharp text as he could.

But as Mark edited, we differed, and I began to add stuff back in. In a sense something as verbally dense and rich as *Henry IV* needs it all or it needs nothing, and the piece became misshapen. We fought, and there's nothing as demoralising as fighting with your collaborator and best friend. During a run through midway through rehearsals Mark walked out. The relationship between a director and a writer can be fraught with ego. It wasn't exactly a wounded Will Shakespeare who exited mid-run but it was the next best thing. I rang him and we made up, agreeing, among other things, that we needed to make the sword fights as spectacular as possible.

In the end we were both really pleased with *Henry*. It was a piece about friendship, tall tales and father/son anxiety, and the tension between the environment you inhabit versus the one you inherit. It opened in the Peacock and had brilliant performances from Declan Conlon, Sean Kearns, Niamh Linehan, Nick Dunning and a haunted, complex portrayal of Hal by the late Tom Murphy. Over all it was well received but the Abbey didn't pick up the mantle for us to do *Part II*, which is a shame because we were definitely onto something.

In 2006 I got my chance to work on *Howie the Rookie* in a production at the Peacock Theatre, the first time the play was produced at the Abbey. I enjoyed every minute of it. I loved being in its verbal embrace. But I was using the same actors – Aidan Kelly and Karl Shiels who had performed in the original production – and I felt like I couldn't bring anything substantially new to the play. I liked the idea that Karl and Aidan were having a last go; like ageing gunslingers in a Sam Peckinpah Western on one last, insane, job. It gave the production a vaguely elegiac air which seemed entirely appropriate. Things were changing.

Mark was also eager to direct his own work at this stage. In his early work, he sought to contain the damage a director could bring to his work by limiting it to monologues, creating a confined space, where it is an actor speaking Mark's words that create the imaginary, and there isn't much room for misinterpretation.

We talked about directing all the time. About what we liked and didn't care for. When it boiled right down to it our only difference was I liked more movement on stage then he did. But even then we'd probably argue with each other the other way too.

He got the opportunity to direct his own work with *Terminus*, which was produced at the Peacock in 2007, and presented three very different but deeply dark stories, in verse!! About a year previously Mark said he wanted to tell me the story, to see if it held together, and in a cafe on Wicklow Street, over about 40 minutes, he held steady eye contact and relayed this tender tale of devil-riding gore, full of slashing death and a mother's love, while other punters looked on in open-mouthed horror. I could see them thinking: 'what is this madman saying?' But the story held you glued and the horror thrills were deserved.

As Mark's confidence grows as a director his scope for staging expands. He recently revisited *Howie the Rookie* with a towering performance by Tom Vaughan Lawlor, who showed a remarkable zeal for Mark's language in an almost acrobatic staging. It established the play, finally, as a modern classic. Mark once saw a kid in Eason's bookshop nick a copy of *Howie the Rookie* off the shelves, and was filled with pride, while being slightly miffed at the loss of royalties: it was a classic if it was worth nicking.

Mark recently told me the scenario for his next play. It's a family drama tinged with horror that requires an epic visual sensibility. He was struggling with two different ways of telling the story, and he wanted to test which was the most effective. I gasped at one way; that helped him make his decision, he said. It premiered under Mark's direction last year in the Abbey: Mark has become his own best storyteller.

2 | 'Keep the Aspidistra Flying': The Satirizing of Celtic Tiger, 'Aspirational' Lifestyles in Mark O'Rowe's Early Work

David S. Clare

In recent years, Fintan O'Toole and other commentators have alleged that Irish writers have shirked the responsibility of capturing and critiquing the changing Ireland within which they live. O'Toole is particularly appalled by the fact that Irish writers have not written more explicitly about Celtic Tiger greed and corruption. It is certainly true that, over the past fifteen years, many – or, indeed, most – of the major works produced by Ireland's celebrated playwrights and fiction writers have been set in pre-Celtic Tiger Ireland, or (more worrying still) in an Ireland that seems quite unlike the one that we inhabit today.[1] This tendency to look back may be due to future shock – that is, Irish writers may have found it difficult to describe such a rapidly changing environment. On the other hand, it may simply be because great literary works are often born out of an author's memory. After all, Joyce's *Ulysses* (1922), like Beckett's *Company* (1980) and Friel's *Dancing at Lughnasa* (1990), did appear before the public many years after the autobiographical incidents they describe.

Against this trend of 'hiding' in the past, Irish writers for film and television have been much happier to dissect contemporary Ireland – both its economic boom and bust, and its rapidly changing culture and demographics. Screenplays and series written for television which

---

[1] My assertions in this opening paragraph apply only to celebrated *individuals* who write plays and literary fiction; I am fully aware that companies who make devised theatre, such as Corn Exchange, Anú Productions, Brokentalkers, and TheatreClub have consistently engaged with contemporary issues in recent years.

vividly capture (and archly comment upon) Celtic Tiger Ireland include Mark O'Halloran's *Adam and Paul* (2004) and *Garage* (2007); John Carney's *Bachelor's Walk* (2001-2003) and *Once* (2007) – the former co-written with Kieran Carney and Tom Hall; Eugene O'Brien's *Pure Mule* (2005-2009); and Michael McElhatton and Ian Fitzgibbon's *Paths to Freedom* (2000). Another such work is the brilliant screenplay to the 2003 film *Intermission*, written by Mark O'Rowe. The fact that this screenplay makes incisive observations about boom-time Dublin should come as little surprise; by the time of the film's release, O'Rowe had already demonstrated that he was one of the few playwrights of his generation interested in confronting contemporary Ireland. O'Rowe's first four major plays – *The Aspidistra Code* (1995), *From Both Hips* (1997), *Howie The Rookie* (1999) and the vastly underappreciated *Made In China* (2001) – clearly reveal that he was inspired, rather than intimidated by, the new energies present in the country. O'Rowe began writing in 1994, and his early work also includes pieces written for Tallaght Youth Theatre and Dublin Youth Theatre, such as *Sulk* and *Buzzin' to Bits* (both 1996), and a one-act monologue about a snuff film director entitled *Anna's Ankle*, which was staged by Bedrock Productions at the Project Arts Centre in 1997. The play *Rundown* was written in 1996, but was not produced until New York's Origin Theatre Company took it on in 2002.

As critics routinely point out, O'Rowe's work is deeply informed by his Tallaght working-class background. However, while such critics frequently dwell upon the ways in which this background informs O'Rowe's language, settings and depictions of masculinity (see, for example, Jordan, Madden, Raab, Singleton and Trotter), they have underestimated the degree to which his work deals explicitly with issues around social class. In O'Rowe's Celtic Tiger-era work, he repeatedly examines the unthinking, as well as the conscious, adoption of middle-class 'aspirational' lifestyles by many Irish people during the boom. Indeed, in the early plays *The Aspidistra Code* and *From Both Hips* – accurately described by their creator as 'kitchen-sink-crime-comedy-drama[s]' (Foreword vii) – and the screenplay to *Intermission*, O'Rowe notes and satirizes the extreme behaviour indulged in by Irish people fixated on 'keeping up with the Joneses' or emulating the people found in Anglo-American visual and print media. Some of O'Rowe's boom-time characters are actually willing to risk their lives in order to acquire (or retain) certain 'middle-class' material possessions, and many of them are happily trading their distinctly Irish way of life for a more homogenized, Western existence, changing the products they buy, as well as the way they speak.

While O'Rowe considers himself (and is considered by others) an 'apolitical' writer (Personal Interview),[2] his depiction of Celtic Tiger 'aspirational' lifestyles is undoubtedly satirical. The definition of 'satire' is hotly contested, but a helpful recent definition comes from critic Jill E. Twark:

> Satirical humour is produced when humor is directed pointedly or aggressively against an object to illustrate its flaws or to censure it in some way. Satire may serve to teach or uplift morally. (Twark 14)

In *The Aspidistra Code*, *From Both Hips*, and *Intermission*, the humour that O'Rowe generates at the expense of characters struggling to become globalized, conformist, middle-class, Western citizens clearly indicates his negative feelings about the foolhardy choices they make.

During the boom, O'Rowe was fascinated by the fact that so many Irish people (from all class backgrounds) were going to great lengths to gain the totems of Western, middle-class success. When I interviewed O'Rowe in 2008 (at the start of the downturn), he said that during the Celtic Tiger, there was intense social pressure to attain these items, because without them, you weren't considered 'a fully-fledged adult.' Although September 2008 is often thought of as the start of the downturn, Irish house prices and tax revenue began to drop steadily from March 2007. These developments, combined with the onset of the U.S. financial crisis in August 2007, meant that, by the time I interviewed O'Rowe in March 2008, he and I were both aware that the boom was over. He noted that Irish people seemed to 'buy into this peer pressure completely, without questioning it.' (Personal Interview) These sentiments echo those of other Irish commentators during the boom. As Colin Coulter lamented in 2003:

> Over the last generation, the Republic of Ireland has, like other western societies, become a place that elevates having over being. It would seem, increasingly, that the principal way in which most southern Irish people are willing or able to express their sense of who they are is through the commodity form. (Coulter 25)

In O'Rowe's breakthrough play *The Aspidistra Code* (first produced as a rehearsed reading on The Abbey Theatre's Peacock stage in

---

[2] Gerry Stembridge, who directed the rehearsed reading of *From Both Hips* at the Peacock and the Abbey production of *Made in China*, has also commented on the apolitical nature of O'Rowe's writing. (As quoted in Lilian Chambers et al 463).

December 1995) and the IFTA-winning screenplay *Intermission*, he contends that simply purchasing commodities associated with 'adulthood' and 'sophistication' does not actually indicate maturity or taste in the consumer. I consider *The Aspidistra Code* a Celtic Tiger-era work, because, according to most economists, the boom started in 1994. In fact, Ireland's economy was first referred to as the 'Celtic Tiger' by Kevin Gardiner (an investment banker working at Morgan Stanley in London) in August of that year (Coulter 3). In this play, the dangerous loan shark Drongo is redecorating his apartment to Celtic Tiger standard, complete with wooden floors and a Persian rug. Far from believing himself a cretin, Drongo regards himself as a 'bohemian' (*Plays: One* 51), who has a taste for poetry and who previously refused to smoke anything but Gauloises and Gitanes. Likewise, the gangster Lehiff from *Intermission* is interested in purchasing some of the trappings of middle-class refinement, including a juicer, a wok, and extra virgin olive oil. As O'Rowe indicates in each work, however, changing these surfaces does not alter the fact that these men are anything but refined as people; in fact, they are violent maniacs with no moral 'code'. (*Plays: One* 63; 70) A clear analogy can be drawn between these criminals and the 'gangsters' in all walks of life during the Celtic Tiger (such as bankers and developers), who merely took on the appearance of 'civility', but who were, in fact, selfish and even more of a danger to society than Drongo and Lehiff.

Like Drongo and Lehiff, sympathetic working-class characters in these two works also attempt to rise socially by obtaining, or holding onto, the items often associated in America and Britain with a prosperous, middle-class lifestyle. In *The Aspidistra Code*, Brendan and Sonia, who owe Drongo money, are willing to risk their lives to hold onto an antique chair and an aspidistra plant that the loan shark wants for his Celtic Tiger pad. Antiques have the reputation of conferring 'middle-class respectability' on those whose class status is suspect, or on those whose families have only recently risen in the world. As such, Sonia wants to hold on to the chair, not only because it may be monetarily valuable but also because it confirms that her family is from a higher social class than her present circumstances might suggest. Drongo desires the chair because it will help him to mimic those who come from 'old money'.

With regards to Brendan's beloved aspidistras, they have long been associated with 'middle-class respectability' in the British and Irish literary traditions. In the novel *Keep the Aspidistra Flying* (1938), George Orwell's hero, Gordon, comes to view the aspidistra as 'a symbol' of 'lower-middle-class people' attempting to keep themselves 'respectable'. (Orwell 47; 267; 268) He reaches this conclusion after reading *The Ragged Trousered Philanthropists* (1914), by the Dublin socialist author Robert Tressell (real name Robert Noonan). Gordon is struck by Tressell's account of 'the starving carpenter who pawns everything but sticks to his aspidistra.' (Orwell 47) In O'Rowe's play, Brendan foolishly risks the lives of himself, his wife, his brother and his friend, as he tries to hang on to one of the many aspidistras that he has cultivated. For Drongo, the plant will add yet more respectability to his redecorated flat.

Just as Brendan and Sonia risk their lives for the sake of 'middle-class' material possessions, Mick from *Intermission* – a bus driver who recently lost his job – takes to a life of crime in order to 'keep up with the Joneses'. He plans to use the money he earns from a tiger-kidnapping to keep acquiring items like a new garden shed and 'lovely oak' flooring for his home. (*Intermission*) Mick, like Drongo and Lehiff, desires to partake in the new, prosperous Ireland, and part of that is having a lovely house finished to a 'high spec'. According to O'Rowe, Mick is driven to obtain the garden shed and the wooden flooring not because he likes them personally, but because 'his wife is pushing for them. She thinks having these things will make them the perfect couple.' (Personal Interview) A wife pushing a nonplussed husband to obtain such items is one that O'Rowe claims he often noted among couples of his acquaintance during the boom, and he thought it would be interesting to include that dynamic in his screenplay. (Personal Interview) In bowing to pressure from his wife, Mick (like Brendan and Sonia in *The Aspidistra Code*) jeopardizes his very existence; this is O'Rowe's comment on the fact that many Irish people took foolish risks during the Celtic Tiger (including jeopardizing their financial futures) in order to rise economically and appear as wealthy as their neighbours.

The materialism evident in these working-class characters is nothing compared to that of Sam, the middle-class bank manager from *Intermission*. Sam, no longer fettered by the religious and legal constraints of decades past, decides that he deserves more out of life and leaves his wife of fourteen years for a younger woman. As O'Rowe pointed out to me, there were men during the Celtic Tiger who believed they had 'everything' – a good job, a nice house, a new car. In their minds, all that was 'missing' was a beautiful, young wife, so Sam 'trades in his old wife for a younger model' (Personal Interview) – a common enough story in the rest of the Western world but new for Ireland. Even more tellingly, Sam (in O'Rowe's words) is 'not too angsty about it'.

(Personal Interview) Indeed, he tells his wife that he simply fell in love with another woman so she doesn't 'come into the equation'. (*Intermission*) O'Rowe is suggesting through this character that 'Catholic Ireland is dead and gone' (including the famous, guilty, Catholic conscience). While many might see this as a good thing for Irish society as a whole, Sam's lack of moral conscience and his Celtic Tiger selfishness are chilling, especially when, late in the film, he decides to preserve his own life (and his job) by not complying with the tiger-kidnappers' demands, thus risking his new lover's life.

In O'Rowe's second major play *From Both Hips* (first produced by Fishamble Theatre Company in 1997 in Dublin and Glasgow) and his film *Intermission*, the desire to appear prosperous and worldly leads characters to change their accents and/or to culturally 'sell out' their Irishness. In *From Both Hips*, the Drugs Squad detective, Willy, is distressed by the 'fake-newsreader voice' that his therapist, Dr. Kielty, puts on, which 'sounds kind of English'. (*Plays: One* 106; 105) It stands in sharp contrast to what Willy knows the man's real (or normal) accent to be. Dr. Kielty's 'RTÉ newsreader accent' (*Plays: One* 159) is clearly part of his attempt to appear to be from a higher social class than he actually is. While this irritates Willy, his wife, Irene, discounts her husband's criticisms of the therapist, perhaps because she also desires to portray herself as being from a higher class background. When she finds Willy in what is described in the stage directions as the 'normal, working-class house' that belongs to Paul (a man he accidentally shot while on duty), his wife asks, 'What are you doing here with *these people?*' (*Plays: One* 79; 160, emphasis mine) It is a moment pregnant with class snobbery. Tellingly, the social class standing of Willy and Irene's house is elided in the script.

Willy's nemesis, Paul, is proud to be working-class and (unusually for these works) scorns attempts by others to deviate from the Dublin working-class norms in which they were raised. For example, he considers the Drug Squad's habit of celebrating with 'curries' instead of 'pints' to be a sign of their 'elitist' attitude. (*Plays: One* 142) (The introduction of curries into the Drug Squad's routine is O'Rowe's acknowledgement that Ireland was becoming more open to international cuisine during the mid-1990s – especially as people from the Asian subcontinent began to move to the country in significant numbers. Since Paul is a relatively unsympathetic character, his resistance to this new cultural trend could carry the taint of racism.) Most 'elitist' of all, in Paul's mind, is the Drug Squad's tendency to regard everyone in poorer, working-class areas as criminal. Even though Willy likes people to be 'down to earth' (unlike his wife), he is included in Paul's criticisms of the Drug Squad. When Willy asks Paul what he was doing in the rough neighbourhood where he was shot, Paul replies:

> I told you before, a mate of mine lives there. The whole block isn't criminal. See, it's this kind of attitude, now... You think you can judge these innocent people who don't have the money to live anywhere else? (*Plays: One* 140)

While Paul may differ from other characters in these works in that he is resisting the Celtic Tiger pressure to appear 'middle-class', he is similar to them in that, at the same time, he is happily allowing himself to be transformed by globalized, consumer culture (as his use of the American term 'block' – cited above – indicates). Paul is fascinated by the degree to which Willy's work on the Drugs Squad conforms to the violent fantasies associated with the American police dramas he loves. His speech is peppered with American television and film references. He compares Willy unfavourably to 'Don Johnson' from *Miami Vice*; he refers to Willy as 'the man who shot Liberty Valence'; and he describes himself after the shooting as being 'filled with hot lead'. (*Plays: One* 137, 147; 157; 146) O'Rowe suggests that the incorporation of corny lines from American Westerns, gangster films and television is common across Irish culture. We are told that the gangster Maurice Joyce yelled 'Youse'll never take me alive!' when running from the Drug Squad; Liz talks about Willy and Paul going '*mano a mano*' and tells Theresa that their secret code word should be 'Geronimo'; and, finally, when Willy proposes that Paul shoot him in the leg (as reparation for the accidental shooting), he taunts Paul, saying: 'Are you man enough to dish it out?' (*Plays: One* 144; 160; 169; 164) As O'Rowe commented to me in a public interview I conducted with him at NUI Galway in February 2013, all Irish people may soon be speaking in accents and with syntax that he describes as 'Hiberno-American'. (Public Interview)

Most of O'Rowe's characters have unconsciously started to use Americanisms in their everyday speech, and O'Rowe seems to regard this as, to some degree, inevitable and not terribly serious. (Among his characters, only Hugh from *Made in China* is actively resisting the introduction of Americanisms into Irish speech; he repeatedly criticizes Paddy for using the word 'pants' instead of 'trousers'. (*Plays: One* 233, 240-241)) However, in the case of two characters from *Intermission* – the Garda detective Jerry Lynch and the supermarket manager Mr. Henderson – the process of 'Americanization' brought about by Ireland's engagement with the forces of 'globalization' is much more profound and, to O'Rowe's mind, troubling. Lynch lives as though he actually is a character on an American police drama. He brings a fierce commitment to his job that is reminiscent of the ruthlessly pragmatic and overly intense policemen frequently found in such programmes, and it is hinted that Lynch's job in Dublin does not actually warrant such intensity. As Lynch delivers his terse put-downs of the criminals and fellow cops he encounters, his accent (as portrayed by a riveting Colm Meaney) flattens out and takes on a Yankee twang. Blind to the cultural sell-out so prevalent in the rest of his life, Lynch is convinced that he has the 'requisite Celtic soul' to appreciate the internationally successful CDs produced by 'Celtic Mysticism' artists like Clannad. (*Intermission*) While many might assume that Lynch's love of this music is a sign of his Irish pride, O'Rowe suggested to me that Lynch's perspective on Irish culture is 'almost the view of an outsider'. (Personal Interview) He loves the Irish music that the rest of the world appreciates and sees as mystically Celtic, not what Irish people themselves regard as excellent and authentic. Re-assessing Lynch's character with this in mind, one can see that even Lynch's self-esteem as an Irishman is built around what America thinks is 'cool'.

Lynch is not alone in the film in having an eye cast towards America. John and Oscar's boss, Mr. Henderson, repeatedly uses Americanisms with obvious relish, always following them with the phrase 'as they say in the States'. (*Intermission*) Those he is speaking to are meant to be bowled over by the authority given to his words by their American provenance. The idea that something American is inherently better, or should be given more weight, is reminiscent of Martin McDonagh's lampooning of the national inferiority complex in *The Cripple of Inishmaan* (1997) – a play in which the characters repeatedly say things like 'Ireland musn't be such a bad place so if the Yanks want to come [here] to do their filming.' (McDonagh 8)

During the Celtic Tiger, as Irish people struggled to come to terms with how to be 'successful' (in the Western, materialistic sense of the word), they often looked to the models of success and behaviour that they saw coming from American film and television, and from British lifestyle programmes and Sunday newspaper supplements. This was perhaps understandable, given the fact that they were standing on new ground (and perhaps embarrassed to be so unsure of themselves). However, even though Ireland was culturally enriched during this time by the arrival of the New Irish (the immigrants who came to the country during the boom from Africa, Eastern Europe and Asia), the society-wide tendency to unthinkingly buy into Western, globalized, consumer culture undoubtedly diminished the nation's cultural distinctiveness. This willingness to 'sell out' to Western globalized culture was an abrupt shift from attitudes in pre-boom Ireland, as we shall see.

During the late 1980s and early 1990s, much of the excitement around being Irish stemmed from the belief that (in Roddy Doyle's famous phrase) 'the Irish are the blacks of Europe'. (Doyle et. al.)³ The connections between Ireland and the developing world made by postcolonial critics such as Declan Kiberd, playwrights such as Brian Friel, filmmakers such as Bob Quinn, and musicians from rockers like U2 and Sinéad O'Connor to proto-'Nu Trad' artists like Dónal Lunny and the Afro-Celt Sound System breathed new life into Irish art. The daring, culturally-hybrid works produced out of the (admittedly reductive) belief that Ireland was, in essence, a Third World country led people across the world to see Irishness as a form of 'enriched whiteness' (to borrow a concept from Diane Negra). (Negra 1) As prosperity (and actual non-whites) came to the country, however, many Irish people no longer wanted to emphasize their downtrodden, troubled history or to take pride in the cultural and political similarities that Ireland shares with countries in Asia, Africa and Latin America. They traded 'enriched whiteness', or their status as 'soulful' whites, for the ordinary, conformist, middle-class, prosperous whiteness associated with the majority populations of Western Europe and 'developed' Anglophone countries such as the United States, Canada, Australia and New Zealand. A good example of this shift is the phenomenon highlighted by Patrick Lonergan in his important study, *Theatre and Globalization: Irish Drama in the Celtic Tiger Era* (2009). Here, Lonergan shows that a desire to succeed on the global stage led many Irish playwrights during the boom to produce work that catered to the expectations of the global marketplace. They either depicted Ireland as a 'normal', prosperous, developed country, or they deliberately included elements in their work that they knew international audiences had come to expect from an 'Irish' play. (In other words, they commodified 'Irishness').

One of the reasons why O'Rowe is one of the most important Irish writers of his generation is because he has highlighted and critiqued the nation's move away from dynamic and fruitful artistic dialogue with 'non-white' cultures and towards bland, globalized, Western 'whiteness'. As shown above, in his early work, he mocks Irish people

---

3 This quote comes from *The Commitments* screenplay, which Roddy Doyle co-wrote with Dick Clement and Ian La Frenais. In Doyle's original novel, the quote is slightly different (the 'n-word' is used) (Doyle 13).

who, during the boom, sought to jettison their cultural baggage and to ignore their actual, personal, socio-economic histories. In particular, he pointed up the absurdity of trading one's culturally rich Irish background for an ersatz American or neutered British identity. In these early scripts (including ones not covered in detail in this essay), he suggests that, while the American and British cultures can certainly be inspiring, there is also much to be gained from engagement with non-European cultures. The characters in *The Aspidistra Code*, *From Both Hips*, *Howie the Rookie* and *Made in China* repeatedly reference martial arts, Asian cinema and Thai culture. In *Howie the Rookie*, 'Ladyboy''s nickname is clearly a reference to the ladyboys of Bangkok, and we are told that his Betta fighting fish (spelled 'Beta' in the play) come from 'Siam, which is Thailand' (205). In reference to the indigenous peoples of North and South America, the Native American chiefs Crazy Horse and Geronimo are name-checked (after a fashion) in *The Aspidistra Code* and *From Both Hips*, respectively. In *Howie the Rookie*, the Rookie Lee and his father subscribe to Mayan spiritual beliefs. Finally, in *Made in China*, Native Americans and the Irish are subtly linked when Hugh explains to Paddy that the clothing designer John Rocha looks like 'an [American] Indian' but is, in fact, 'Irish' (232). O'Rowe himself is known to quote his hero Bruce Lee during public appearances. (Pre-Show Talk; Public Interview) Of course, it must be admitted that, as much as the characters in *Howie the Rookie* and *Made in China* admire – and are even obsessed by – exciting aspects of non-European cultures, they also unreflectively use racist epithets like 'Paki', 'Chink', and 'Gook'. (*Plays: One* 188; 205, 249, 250, 256, 294, 295, 296; 250, 257, 296) This is presumably because they are disenfranchised males, who believe that being crudely racist will enhance their 'hard man' image. This same desire to look 'hard' may be behind Paul's (possibly racist) disparagement of curries in *From Both Hips*.

An Irish writer taking inspiration from 'non-white' cultures is certainly not new. W.B. Yeats was inspired by Japanese Noh drama and Indian writers like Rabindranath Tagore. Samuel Beckett's exposure to North Africa can be detected in works such as *Not I* (1972). Going further back, Frances Sheridan, Thomas Moore, and James Clarence Mangan all wrote works that drew on Middle Eastern literature.

In Mark O'Rowe's case, I would contend that the inspiration from 'non-white' cultures extends beyond his love for martial arts and Asian cinema (often cited by critics as important influences on his work) (see, for example, Jordan 345). In Noel Ignatiev's landmark study, *How the*

Irish Became White (1995), he demonstrates that, for many years, the Irish in America were regarded as non-white or, at least, not-quite-white. The same was true of Jewish immigrants to the United States and Britain (see Painter 77, 192, 202). All three of the writers that O'Rowe claims to admire most – David Mamet, Harold Pinter, and Samuel Beckett – come from these marginalized, not-quite-white backgrounds. Their imprint is easily detectable in O'Rowe's work, and not just in his use of beats and pauses. For example, the 'tough-guy back-and-forth' in plays like *Made in China* clearly derives from Mamet's early work. Likewise, there is a brilliant Pinteresque power shift during the highly entertaining *tête-à-tête* between Paul and Willy at the start of Act Two in *From Both Hips*.

Another Jewish influence on O'Rowe (and one that has been strangely ignored by critics) is the work of the Coen Brothers. As O'Rowe admitted to me during the public interview at NUIG, he has seen their 1990 film *Miller's Crossing* 'over sixty times', and it informed his depiction of an Irish male who is reluctant to share his feelings and desires in *Intermission*. Indeed, a key line that Verna says to Tom in *Miller's Crossing* is paraphrased by Deirdre when confronting John towards the end of *Intermission*: 'You always take the long way around to get what you want; don't you, Tom?... You could have just asked.' (Coen Brothers) I would suggest that the influence of *Miller's Crossing* can also be seen in *The Aspidistra Code*. The discussions between Crazy Horse, Drongo and Joe about 'ethics', 'principles' and a criminal 'code' recall similar discussions initiated by Caspar in the Coen Brothers' film. (*Plays: One* 40, 63; 40, 51; 70, 71)

Ultimately, one of the most important connections between O'Rowe and his Jewish and Irish heroes is their treatment of social class. The concern that O'Rowe has for those on the financial margins is also a feature in many of the writers that shaped his imagination, including the works of Beckett, Mamet, and Pinter, as can a similar sensitivity to cross-class power dynamics and the perils of social climbing. We can only be grateful that O'Rowe maintained this perspective during the Celtic Tiger, a time when greed was causing Irish people to forget their personal and national pasts and to pursue blindly dubious personal and financial goals. During the boom, O'Rowe reminded Irish people of where they had been and questioned where they were going.

In particular, he satirized Celtic Tiger 'aspirational' lifestyles, challenging those Irish people who were trading 'enriched whiteness' for bland, conformist, materialistic, Western 'whiteness'. O'Rowe's willingness to hold a mirror up to the Irish people (both during the boom and after) is unusual among contemporary, Irish writers of drama and literary fiction; it is also one of the most important – if under recognized – aspects of O'Rowe's excellent and entertaining work.

Works Cited

Chambers, Lillian, Ger Fitzgibbon and Eamonn Jordan, eds. *Theatre Talk: Voices of Irish Theatre Practitioners*. Dublin: Carysfort Press, 2001.

Coen, Joel and Ethan. Screenplay to *Miller's Crossing*. Dir. Joel Coen. Twentieth Century Fox, 1990.

Coulter, Colin. "The End of Irish History?" *The End of Irish History?: Critical Reflections on the Celtic Tiger*. Eds. Colin Coulter and Steve Coleman. Manchester: Manchester University Press, 2003. 1-33.

Doyle, Roddy, Dick Clement and Ian La Frenais. Screenplay to *The Commitments*. Dir. Alan Parker. Twentieth Century Fox, 1991.

---. *The Barrytown Trilogy: The Commitments / The Snapper / The Van*. London: Penguin, 1995.

Jordan, Eamonn. 'Urban Drama: Any Myth Will Do?'. *The Dreaming Body: Contemporary Irish Theatre*. Eds. Melissa Sihra and Paul Murphy. Gerrards Cross: Colin Smythe, 2009. 15-17.

Madden, Ed. "Exploring Masculinity: Proximity, Intimacy and Chicken". *Irish Masculinities: Reflections on Literature and Culture*. Eds. Caroline Magennis and Raymond Mullen. Dublin: Irish Academic Press, 2011. 82-83.

McDonagh, Martin. *The Cripple of Inishmaan*. London: Methuen, 1997.

Negra, Diane. "The Irish in Us: Irishness, Performativity and Popular Culture". *The Irish in Us*. Ed. Diane Negra. Durham, NC: Duke University Press, 2006. 1-19.

O'Rowe, Mark. Foreword. *Plays: One*. By Mark O'Rowe. London: Nick Hern Books, 2011. vii-x.

---. Personal Interview. Eason's Cafe, Dublin. 12 March 2008.

---. *Plays: One*. London: Nick Hern Books, 2011.

---. Pre-Show Talk before *Crestfall*, by Mark O'Rowe. The Gate Theatre, Dublin. 30 May 2003.

---. Public Interview conducted by David Clare. The Moore Institute Seminar Room, NUI Galway. 25 February 2013.

---. Screenplay to *Intermission*. Dir. John Crowley. Buena Vista, 2003.

Orwell, George. *The Complete Works of George Orwell*, Volume Four: Keep the Aspidistra Flying. Ed. Peter Davison. London: Secker & Warburg, 1987.

Painter, Nell Irwin. *The History of White People*. New York: W.W. Norton, 2011.

Raab, Michael. "Mark O'Rowe". *The Methuen Guide to Contemporary Irish Playwrights*. Eds. Martin Middeke and Peter Paul Shnierer. London: Methuen, 2010. 351, 355

Singleton, Brian. *Masculinities and the Contemporary Irish Theatre*. Houndmills: Palgrave Macmillan, 2011. 79-80.

Trotter, Mary. *Modern Irish Theatre*. Cambridge: Polity Press, 2008. 183-184.

Twark, Jill E. *Humor, Satire, and Identity: Eastern German Literature in the 1990s*. Berlin: de Gruyter, 2007.

3 | Expletive Narrative: Mark O'Rowe's *Howie the Rookie*: Early Critical Reception of Dublin's Dark Diegetic Narrative

Thomas B. Costello

Howie the Rookie is a play that deserves special attention in terms of its narration. While there may be other plays which share the two act, two monologue layout, the form remains unusual in contemporary theatre. Playwright Mark O'Rowe uses a direct, present tense narration from the first-person point of view throughout *Howie the Rookie,* and his narrative style has radically shaped how critics have engaged with the play in production. Further, the highly stylized and 'authentic' urban vernacular employed by O'Rowe has been the point of much discussion and, consequently, this particular play/playwright combination makes for an invigorating discussion of the implied author as applied to modern drama. The English professor and narrative theorist Brian Richardson has published compelling work on both diegetic narration and implied authorship, thus this article will employ Richardson's theoretical framework as a springboard to dive beneath theatrical reviews and tease out some of what makes O'Rowe's richly narrative play – and its playwright – so successful.

To first contextualize the play and its form, consider how critic Ben Brantley introduces readers to *Howie the Rookie*. In his review for the *New York Times*, Brantley consciously foregrounds O'Rowe's use of language by crafting his review with an urgency similar to that found in the play:

> Mr. O'Rowe's writing has itchy feet; like the characters it portrays, it can't stand still. [...] The play is ripe with propulsive syntax, musical repetitions and majestic hyperbole that somehow keep speech on a gut level of engagement. (Brantley)

Brantley found it necessary to introduce O'Rowe to a wider audience with such vivid language because the emergent playwright was bringing something very new, and perhaps unsettling, to the stage.

Mark O'Rowe burst onto the popular theatre scene in 1999 with a shocking dual-monologue thriller entitled *Howie the Rookie*. Critics were quick to take note: O'Rowe was another fresh, young Irish playwright to emerge from the turbulence of the Celtic Tiger with a knack for writing powerful monologue, and he was using this talent to bring life to a section of Ireland which has been largely kept away from the stage, and indeed away from the theatres as well. *Howie the Rookie* captured the violent and harsh underbelly of contemporary Dublin with a rogue Irish poetic narrative hitherto unseen on stage. Not unusual for a contemporary urban writer from Ireland, O'Rowe's watershed play first greeted audiences abroad. It was produced by the Bush Theatre in London, and moved to Dublin only after garnering nearly unanimous critical praise and chalking up a sold-out run at the small London theatre renowned for intimate storytelling. If McDonagh is credited with giving Irish drama a stinging twist of black comedy, than O'Rowe upped the ante considerably with his pointed urban vernacular and ultraviolent tendencies.

Howie the Rookie traces the paths of two young good-for-nothing Dublin hooligans: The Howie Lee and The Rookie Lee. (O'Rowe maintains the capitalized definite articles for his characters throughout the duration of the play.) Although they share the surname 'Lee' – 'as in The Bruce Lee' they note – that is where their similarities end. The two are acquaintances in that they are peers who run in the same crowds, but they aren't quite friends. The Howie Lee is a fighter and The Rookie Lee is a lover. Each character possesses a physique to match their particular prowess; The Howie is rough and has a reputation for dealing out a good beating, and The Rookie is a suave ladies man who doesn't win a lot of fights. The story of the play covers two overlapping days, as detailed in first-person present tense narratives, delivered in turn from the perspective of each Lee.

Act I's monologue belongs to The Howie Lee. He lays out a situation where a friend's mattress seems to have contracted scabies, and consequently he and his friends are out to give the suspected culprit a beating. In order to do so, Howie dodges his babysitting duties to help in the hunt for the poor soul who may or may not have had anything to do with the mattress in the first place. That unfortunate lad is The Rookie Lee, who, as Howie relates, they stalk, catch, and gently pummel. When Howie returns home, he finds his normally distant parents distraught. He then learns that his kid brother 'The Mousie Lee' has wandered out of the house and been run over by a car while Howie was out causing trouble. The parents blame Howie, as he should've been at home watching Mousie to begin with. Despondent, Howie leaves the house, never to return again. So ends the first act.

The second act/monologue is that of The Rookie Lee, and it is somewhat a tangled comedy of violent errors. His story begins with a detailed examination of the bind that he is in; mainly the fact that he owes €700 to a formidable hoodlum who goes by the name 'Ladyboy' and is described as possibly having three rows of teeth, like a shark, along with a penchant for astounding cruelty. It turns out that The Rookie was responsible in part for the death of Ladyboy's prize fighting fish: Ladyboy had them on the street to show off their fighting spirit, and The Rookie accidentally knocked them over while ferociously scratching a sudden itch. Bad luck indeed, and Ladyboy has made it painfully clear that The Rookie will never walk again if he doesn't turn up with big money for replacement fighting fish. As The Rookie is trying to figure out a way to come up with the cash, Howie and crew find him, chase him down, and give him a beating that he doesn't quite understand, all the while, he's getting itchier and itchier. Hours pass, and The Rookie Lee settles into a pub to drown his new injuries and try to figure out how to come up with the necessary blood money. He decides to use the only means he can think of – sexual prowess – so he plots to caress the needed cash out of a previous romantic exploit. That goes poorly when her slow but monstrous brother shows up, and suddenly, The Rookie is being thrashed for the second time that day. Then, seemingly out of nowhere, The Howie Lee appears and saves The Rookie from the beating, and insists upon helping him further. He instructs The Rookie on a topical cream to cure his itching – from the scabies of course – and Howie ultimately stands up to Ladyboy in The Rookie's stead. This penultimate battle of the play, between Howie and Ladyboy, turns out to be an epic free-for-all, the likes of which cause those watching to get sick and faint. O'Rowe's narrative is unfaltering in the description of such graphic violence.

Thus it would seem that in the end, the fatality of young Mousie Lee has given The Howie Lee a new perspective on life, and he is determined to save The Rookie Lee who is, as he continually asserts, his 'namesake in Lee-ness' only (O'Rowe 15). Howie comes to his end not, surprisingly, due to the cataclysmic brawl with Ladyboy, but rather due to the unfortunate and bizarre set of circumstances which immediately follow. Having previously and secretly enjoyed sexual relations with a close friend's large sister – they refer to her only by the nickname 'Avalanche' – Howie is ratted out and his friends look to exact revenge on him for the deed. They locate him collapsed on the floor and recovering from the epic bout with Ladyboy. Too exhausted to move, Howie proves an easy target and his 'friends' throw him out a second storey window where he lands, rather unfortunately, impaled on an iron fence. Still not quite dead yet, The Howie meets his ultimate end only when Flann Dingle, an acquaintance described as 'the essence of stench' (O'Rowe 16), loses control of a green Hiace van which then careers off the road and into the house via the exact spot in the fence where Howie is skewered. Again, O'Rowe's details are like the car wreck they describe, horrific, but far too interesting to ignore. Like The Howie Lee, The Rookie Lee is profoundly moved by his immediate experience of death, and he finally resolves to go and explain the dreadful event to Howie's parents. The play reaches its conclusion with The Rookie Lee sitting in The Howie Lee's parents' living room, with a video of young Howie on the television, staring him in the face.

Of course the catch is, none of this action *happens* in the play – it is merely related during the two monologues. And although the preceding summary may seem extensive, it only scratches the surface of the complex and nightmarish narrative web that O'Rowe has woven. The play is absolutely filled with dramatic action, yet on paper it is simply two long monologues. A brief glance at the page and it looks boring: There is not a single stage direction in the published play, there are no character descriptions, there is nothing but two monologues tempered with some basic line breaks for formatting within. It genuinely questions traditional assumptions of theatrical texts. Like a transcribed one-man-show, the play seems to want to be a short story, or journal, or some sort of urban anthropological evidence. Yet, it lives on the stage. As a story it is somewhat compelling, as a theatrical production it is absolutely fascinating. Not only is it contemporary theatre, but if our critics can be trusted, it is particularly good contemporary theatre.

The reason that this particular play has taken off with such fervour has to do with the way O'Rowe crafts his narrative. *Howie the Rookie* is so striking because O'Rowe manipulates coarse urban vernacular into a living poetry whose beauty is somehow balanced by its acute graphic violence. This holds true even for audiences halfway around the world, for whom a harsh Dublin accent might be wholly foreign and unintelligible. As Stephen Winn puts it in the *San Francisco Chronicle*:

> Howie' creates its own language – the rhythms and imagery, diction and syntax – and teaches the audience to listen. Great

theater grabs us by the ears and demands that we hear, *then* see and feel, the world in its own distinctive key. (Winn, emphasis added)

This is particularly true of *Howie the Rookie*, because the language is the play, and there is no getting away from it. As Winn emphasizes, this is a play to be heard – and as written, that's all there is, two very long monologues. While reviews of the play in various productions around the world might mention direction or design, this is undoubtedly a playwright's play; critical attention is first thrust toward O'Rowe, and only thereafter spread to the actor(s) who have tackled his challenging narrative.

O'Rowe's Violent Tense and Offensive POV: Presently Horrific

The first and most obvious tool in O'Rowe's playwriting toolbox is the present tense. Although we have come to expect theatre to happen in the present – that is, after all, its most defining element, that it happens presently in front of an audience – O'Rowe's particular mode of present tense theatrical storytelling is unusual. O'Rowe throws audiences directly into the action via a distinctly urban Dublin tongue:

> A man ahead, some fuck standin' there, stick in his hand, proddin' whatever's burnin'. Makin' sure it all goes up.
> Me, The Howie Lee, getting' closer now.
> Passin' through the field, me way home.
> Field, the back of the flats there, back of Ollie's flat, me mate Ollie's an', Jesus, it *is* Ollie, little fire built, he's standin' there, watchin' it, one hand in his pocket, now an' again, stick prods the burnin'... whatsit?
> What *is* it?
>
> Come close. All right, Ollie?
> All right, The Howie?
> Stop, stand, cock me tush.
> The fuck're you burnin'?
> Me mat, he says. (O'Rowe 7)

Thus, in just half of the first page, and with very few words, The Howie has introduced himself, his buddy Ollie, and the burning mat that will be the first domino in a series of escalating action. He also presents the container for such action, a heady urban lingo unbound by traditional spelling or grammatical constraints. It is a challenge the audience must rise to meet, as is the urgency presented by the relentless present tense.

In what has become a widely syndicated article, *Remembrance of Tense Past,* Lynne Schwartz points out what she perceives as the many pitfalls of using the present tense in storytelling. Specifically she notes that the 'novelty' of the present tense is a dangerous lure, and that it asks too much of a reader, such that 'besides everything else, readers are asked to believe the story is happening as they read' (Schwartz 16). While her assertion applies primarily to fictional literature,[4] this claim can similarly be put up against O'Rowe's drama, as it does make big demands of its audience. There is an inherent irony at hand in a play such as *Howie the Rookie,* where audiences are asked to believe that a tremendous amount of action is happening presently, and yet none of it is physically being played out on stage in front of them.

In that way, the play harkens back to storytelling traditions, where the audience is on a journey with the storyteller, yet tasked with imagining the dramatic action inside their heads at the same time. To be sure, this is the primary task that O'Rowe is charging his audiences with. This in itself is interesting, and even more so in the fact that we're given the story not by one narrator, but rather directly by the two characters who live the story. In this instance, the first person, present tense narrative delivers. Jason Zinoman's later review in the *New York Times* (2005) follows Brantley's lead by focusing again on the 'propulsive' language, figuratively demonstrating how O'Rowe's usage of person/tense makes the play both effective and unique:

> What makes it stand out from the legions of other crime stories is its idiosyncratic language, a propulsive stream of muscular verbs and baroque slang spoken in the first person and present tense. It was almost as if Mr. O'Rowe had studied Samuel Beckett's chiseled prose and Martin McDonagh's outrageous violence and then tried to best them. (Zinoman)

Brian Richardson's article 'Point of View in Drama' reclaims this type of narrative storytelling for the theatre. He dismisses the conventional school of thought that attempts to confine dramatic work exclusively to *mimesis,* and asserts that it is 'difficult to ignore the role of *diegesis* in the drama' (Richardson 194). Although he does not address plays which are as purely narrative as *Howie the Rookie,* he does suggest that '[i]n plays where the narrator has a larger role, other and more perplexing critical conundrums arise' (196). This is certainly

---

[4] She goes on to posit that authors who rely upon the present tense are afraid of developing a distinct voice of their own - certainly a charge that few, if any, would levy against O'Rowe. Indeed, most champion him as having put forth a very distinct voice.

the case with *Howie,* which features two subjective narratives which eschew the traditional presumption that 'dramatic representation is invariably objective, unmediated, devoid of subjectivity' (204). Richardson goes on to offer that:

> It is also the case that the material presence of actors adds a powerful dimension to psychic representation: the instability of the classical idea of an autonomous self is especially persuasive and unnerving when acted out by distinct bodies and voices. (206)

In terms of 'unnerving psychic representation acted out by distinct bodies and voices,' Richardson has got at the major underpinnings of *Howie the Rookie*. The play's defining characteristics are its generally unnerving narrative, incredibly distinct voice, and psychic representation, which collude to ask audiences to embark on a very different type of theatrical journey – and one that is profoundly narrative.

The text presents some considerable problems for an audience looking to dissect the narration. First and foremost, what is going on? In reading a fictional text set in the present tense, all of the problems that Schwartz outlines apply, primarily that a reader has to believe that the action is happening as they read. However in viewing *Howie the Rookie*, this isn't possible. The action can't, really, be happening right now, because the characters in question are on stage telling the story. What is more, both implicitly address the audience directly, explaining things as they go along. To continue the monologue from the first page, Howie goes on:

> Ollie's flat befits a messy cunt like him.
> Kip the night, you kip on the guest mat under an oul' slumberdown. You're a bloke and you're game, you can kip in the bed *with* him. Game meaning gay, neither of which I am, furthest thing from, so I go to the mat. Or did.
> On the mat I kip.
> Did! kipped!
> It's gone now. That's it he's burnin'. (O'Rowe 7, emphasis original)

The Howie's sidebar explaining the sleeping situation at Ollie's is not part of an omniscience the audience has into his soul, rather it is simply him explaining it to clarify his story. So on page one, or in the first two minutes of the play, the audience is presented with the possibility that Howie is telling the story in the present tense, but that it is past action. His brief flustered confusion of tenses seems to confirm this reading of the narrative. However, come the end of the play, Howie is left well and truly dead. This, of course, means that he hasn't lived to tell the story, so what narrative options are an audience left with? Perhaps he was narrating the story posthumously, but such a conclusion would question the palpable urgency of the play. Or could it be that The Howie occupies the elusive position of 'impossible narrative' presented by Richardson in his 1995 treatise 'I etcetera: On the Poetics and Ideology of Multipersoned Narratives' (324). It does seem that both The Howie's and The Rookie's narratives are at least somewhat problematic to anyone attempting to pin them down, or chart them according to reality. In the same article, Richardson sums up the similarly problematic narrative of other modern writers:

> [T]here is often a conflation of waking and dreaming, fantasy and parody, representation and metatheater that makes it impossible to determine effectively just what happened to whom. (Richardson 300)

In this instance, we know generally what happened – Howie died – but we don't have a rational explanation for how it all plays out in the theatre. The interplay between the story and the narrative remains murky under scrutiny. It is a good evening of theatre, and both critics and audiences want to believe something about it, but its break from the conventions of theatrical storytelling leaves open questions as to how these particular characters can be relating this story to us. Or, as Richardson emphasizes 'what many playwrights demonstrate is the overthrowing of law – in particular, the laws of nature' (203). O'Rowe certainly revels in that luxury, not to mention the countless instances of his characters patently disobeying numerous Irish laws all to a comic, if tragic, effect.

Multipersoned Narrative: O'Rowe's Sliding-Scale of Narration and Dialogue

Throughout *Howie the Rookie*, O'Rowe teases the audience with multipersoned narratives. Although he doesn't pursue this facet of the narration to the point of confusion, there is surprisingly little second person speech in the play, direct or indirect. Instead, much of the dialogue is presented in the first person. Take, for instance, this interaction between Howie and his mother:

> Mind your brother. Mind Mousey.
>
> I'm busy.
> Me an' your oul'fella's goin' the fort.
> I'm busy, get out of me face.

> Wears this spangly shit on her cheeks, 'cross her nose, her glasses magnify, make it flash at me, gimme a tense nervous.
>
> I won't get out of your face.
> Leave me alone
> No, I won't. You mind The Mousey Lee.
> No, I won't.
> So forth, enter the oul' fella. (O'Rowe 9)

This exchange is typical of O'Rowe's writing. The second person descriptors of 'she said/says' are omitted, and it isn't always exactly clear when The Howie is quoting speech or narrating. Ultimately the fast and loose narration seems to allow the play to maintain its breakneck pace throughout, with the added benefit of keeping audiences alert. Of course, some of this narrative could translate into action on stage as well, with actors being able to use sections of dialogue as opportunities for first-person re-enactment, without the speedbumps that the addition of 'she says' would present. Consequently when critics describe the piece, they emphasize the urgent collusion of language and action, as Ben Brantley did when he introduced American audiences to the play via the *New York Times* in 2001:

> we're right there with him, running and sweating and breathing hard, and not in the past tense but the present. It's one of those rare, shiver-making instances in which language seems to become truly physical. (Brantley)

The physicalization of dialogue and action is the only way that such a rapidly moving play could remain accessible to audiences. A further complication for *Howie the Rookie* has to do with the extreme Dublin street dialect employed by O'Rowe. While native Irish audiences might be able to follow most of the language without too much difficulty, there is a danger that foreign audiences could get lost amidst O'Rowe's prose. Given the show's success and the vast touring opportunities afforded to it, some reviews speak directly to the concern over how other Anglophone audiences respond to the speech. To continue Stephen Winn's review from the *San Francisco Chronicle*, entitled in regards to dialect:

> It took about 10 minutes, people were saying in the lobby of the Magic Theatre at intermission. That was how long before the first act of 'Howie the Rookie,' a strange and scintillating Irish drama playing through next Sunday, began to click for them. Part of the audience's adjustment has to do with the performer's Irish accent ... a slang- and obscenity-studded Dublin street argot. (Winn)

The title of the theatre review 'Listen Closely, Then See and Feel' demonstrates again the primacy of narrative; this is a play to be heard. Only after an audience consciously accepts the language can O'Rowe's dramatic content come to life. The dialect, violence, and gritty nature of *Howie the Rookie* is echoed throughout O'Rowe's other work as well, and has led many to label him the de facto expert on all the hidden terrors of Dublin.

Implied Authenticity – O'Rowe the Hoodlum?

Perhaps the most interesting overlap between Richardson's narrative theorizing and O'Rowe's playwriting has to do with implied authorship. Although Richardson eventually moves in a different direction with his discussion of implied authorship, he defines the implied author on a basic level as 'not the biographical individual who composed a given work, but an idealized persona who seems to stand between the author and the text' (206). He goes on to declare that this concept can be expanded from literature to the theatre, where 'the audience naturally constructs an image of the figure behind the play which can be very different from the real person who moved the pen across the paper' (206).

In terms of O'Rowe's violent urban drama, Richardson's theorizing could not be truer. Apart from heady comparisons to Joyce,[5] reviews of *Howie the Rookie* often refrain with ideas of authenticity. To borrow from Kevin Manganaro's Broadway.com review of a later (2005) production of *Howie the Rookie* at the Irish Arts Center in New York: 'The buzzword here is 'authentic,' since O'Rowe seems dedicated, for better and for worse, to keeping this slice of life as real as possible' (Manganaro). This theme is echoed in numerous reviews, and *Howie the Rookie* is regularly regarded as an unabridged glimpse into the underbelly of Dublin life, as written by someone who knows. It is touted as authentic almost to the point of voyeurism.

That certainly has something to do with the runaway success of the play – people love a safe glimpse into something so distinctly 'other' and taboo – however the popular sentiment surrounding the play, and indeed its 'implied author' is purely fiction. Although it doesn't sound nearly as appealing in a newspaper review, O'Rowe isn't an impoverished street thug-turned-prize-winning-playwright. He's a very

---

[5] Comparisons with the urban narrative poetry of James Joyce are to be found in several reviews of O'Rowe's work, and would make for a fascinating study in a companion volume, however the subject is beyond the scope of this article.

talented writer who took a liking to renting slasher films as a teenager, and later turned to playwriting 'at 24 'for something to do' after spending his youth acquiring an extensive knowledge of the bloodiest films he could find' (Gibbons).

O'Rowe's youth wasn't spent in a tracksuit on the streets of Dublin, rather he grew up in Tallaght, a working-class suburb south of the city, where his formative years were without significant incident. The primary graphic violence that he experienced in those years was on his television screen, as he indulged in horror films in his spare time. In a 2003 interview with *The Guardian*, O'Rowe describes how he and his friends 'grew up on video nasties, cannibal movies and kung-fu flicks [...] Really we only watched them for the goryness of the special effects' (Gibbons). In doing so throughout his teenage years, he developed a fondness for senseless and grotesque violence:

> I like the feeling that things can turn bad at any time,' he says. 'I never sit down and deliberately plot a point of horror, but if I have a choice between a character being knocked down and killed in the next five minutes or falling in love, I'll usually go for them being run over. (Gibbons)

For audiences attending or reading a play of O'Rowe's, there is a tendency to want to believe it: the implied author of *Howie the Rookie* is surely a worthless urban scoundrel, living day-by-day, fighting for kicks and undaunted by pain. How a character such as this comes to playwriting is anybody's guess, perhaps it was on a whim to earn some cash to reimburse a shark-toothed gangster for his trampled fighting fish?

Although the reviews are nearly unanimous in their praise for the authenticity of O'Rowe's writing, there is a curious disconnect that permeates the criticism surrounding his plays. O'Rowe is also unequivocally commended for his poetry, dynamic storytelling abilities, and the sheer imagination of his fabula. Compressed into a few words, the reviews might distill down to 'unbelievably authentic.' Given the driving urgency of O'Rowe's first person present tense narrative, audiences don't have time to think. However, if they did, the 'authenticity' of O'Rowe's writing would quickly become strained. People, even very mean ones, do not have three rows of teeth, like sharks. The coincidences of his stories are too many, and the horror too perfect. Once an audience digests the material and can critically look back at it the implied author will soon fade away to reveal the true Mark O'Rowe. Of course this is a writer with a vivid imagination and a penchant for horror films; once considered, who else could've written it? But thinking of the playwright as a slasher-film addict is less exciting than believing that *Howie the Rookie* is an authentic living-museum piece accurately depicting a day-in-the-life of two troubled Dublin youths. Audiences might prefer that the play offer some type of grotesque realism, thus the power of the implied author that is subconsciously constructed during the production. Perhaps theatre audiences who buy into the implied author leave the theatre with a better, yet fictional, understanding of the troublesome urban youth that they occasionally glimpse about the city outside the theatre?

As it were, O'Rowe is not an authentic scanger[6] after all, but rather a very good playwright with a frighteningly clever knack for Dublin's urban vernacular. Several plays later, contemporary Irish critics are taking note, not to crush the implied author – that will always remain in the mind of the spectator – but to qualify the authenticity so often ascribed to O'Rowe. As Alan O'Riordan notes in the *Irish Independent*:

> [O'Rowe] has no interest in the gritty realism of urban crime; he takes his inspiration from his native city only verbally. His crime capers, unlikely violent scenarios and rogues galleries of characters are inspired by other writers and directors. He seeks to be not a realist, but something like the Guy Ritchie of Irish theatre. (O'Riordan)

With several plays and films now under his belt it becomes clear that O'Rowe's mastery has to do with so adeptly capturing the language and stylizing his narrative after urban troublemakers. Needless to say, the shock value of using such powerful narrative is high, as is the danger inherent in doing so, and the issue of explicitness is one worth briefly dealing with. *Howie the Rookie* is rife with offensive material, precisely the type of vulgarity that causes young adults to swoon and blush with admiration over the apparent lack of respect for authority. Comparisons with Tarantino are obligatory, however O'Rowe's writing is of a different sort altogether. According to Byron Woods's 2008 review for *Indy Week*:

> [T]he adrenal exhilaration we experience stems from the playwright's bravura street poetry: a buzzy verbal jazz that never fails. O'Rowe has been compared, justifiably, to David Mamet and Quentin Tarantino but, thankfully, Rookie and Howie lack the stagy artifice of the latter and the celebration of mean-spiritedness and misogyny often found in the former. (Woods)

---

[6] 'Scanger' is a pejorative term for troubled urban youth in Ireland, typically linked to pretty criminality and tracksuits. In other words, *scangers* are precisely the type of people that O'Rowe features in *Howie the Rookie*.

Where Tarantino's films are forcibly driven by expletive, O'Rowe's plays are fueled by a specific, and seemingly uncensored, vernacular. While likely to be no less explicit than Tarantino, the language expounded by O'Rowe's characters comes off as justified and earnest. Even the violence in *Howie the Rookie* is more palatable, perhaps because it is necessarily poetic: We don't see it, we only hear about it and the violence itself isn't the spectacle, rather it is the necessary end to an unfortunate, but clear and causally related, string of events.

Richardson concludes one of his articles with the following insight: 'Because theatre is a largely mimetic genre, experiments in staged *diegesis* are all the more daring, powerful, and theoretically challenging' (212). Such a statement could very well begin a review for Mark O'Rowe's *Howie the Rookie*. As a play, it endeavors to exist within the world of *diegesis*, and the action on stage happens in a liminal space between the present tense monologues and the actual presence of the characters. The implied O'Rowe serves to create a fanciful delusion of voyeurism for audiences, and that is perhaps the whole point of this drama. Rather than suffering the suspension-of-disbelief put forth by traditional mimetic theatre, O'Rowe's spectators are transported into a world of belief fueled by 'authentic' urban diegetic narratives. It is daring, powerful, and theoretically challenging, and it works: The implied author lives, and the real audiences swoon.

Works Cited

Brantley, Ben. 'Warrior Heroes Wielding the Power of Words.' *The New York Times* 9 January, 2001.

Gibbons, Fiachra. 'The Dark Stuff.' *The Guardian,* 24 Nov. 2003.

Manganaro, Kevin. 'Howie the Rookie.' *Broadway.com*. Broadway.com, 12 May 2005. Web.

O'Riordan, Alan. "Ritchie' O'Rowe revels in rap, rhythm and rhyme.' *Irish Independent,* 16 June 2007.

O'Rowe, Mark. *Howie the Rookie*. London: Nick Hern Books, 1999.

Richardson, Brian. 'I etcetera: On the Poetics and Ideology of Multipersonal Narratives.' *Style,* 28:3 (1994): 312-328.

Richardson, Brian, 'Point of View in Drama: Diegetic Monologue, Unreliable Narrators, and the Author's Voice on Stage.' *Comparative Drama,* 22:3 (1988): 193-214.

Schwartz, Lynne Sharon. 'Remembrance of Tense Past.' *The Writer* Aug. 1993: 16-19.

Winn, Stephen. 'Listen Closely, Then See and Feel. 'Howie the Rookie' taps the power of vibrant stage language.' *San Francisco Chronicle* 25 Feb. 2001.

Woods, Byron. 'Delta Boys' Howie the Rookie nets rare five-star review: A drop of the hard stuff.' *Indy Week* 12 Mar. 2008.

Zinoman, Jason. 'In Savage Quarters, a Reign of Sex, Violence and Alliteration.' *New York Times* 10 Oct. 2005.

4 | The Small Guy with the Glasses

Aidan Kelly

It was 1998 and we were drinking in The Sackville Lounge. There weren't too many actors in Dublin, less still actors who are working at a particular time, less again actors who get paid for working, but those who were and did drank in The Sackville. A small guy with glasses approached the table I was at. There wasn't much small talk. He had seen me in a show at City Arts Centre – a now-gone jewel of a theatre with the most unfortunate pillar smack bang in the middle of its playing space – and he asked me would I be in a play of his in London. I'm not sure how much choice I would have had, so I just said yes. Sometime later I would get a chance to read the play: *Howie the Rookie*.

First, there was the small obstacle of the director to get past. Mike Bradwell was the Artistic Director of The Bush Theatre in West London, a small greenhouse nursery of a theatre that was then nurturing some of the biggest writers in British drama. He was a larger-than-life character with leopard-print creepers and a red duffle coat who always drained his red wine and would often walk out in the middle of a conversation without saying goodbye. Mike obviously had his own ideas about who should play the two parts in Mark's monologue play because there were a lot of guys lined up to audition, actors with a lot more experience and expertise than me. So it was not quite as clear-cut as being given a straight offer by the playwright. My agent at the time was pushing for another client to do the play; he was a soon to be Hollywood star, and it would have been a platform for his obvious talent and exceptional good looks. It seemed even then that the 'powers-that-be' understood what an exceptional piece of writing they had in their possession, and they wanted the best people in place to perform it to maximum effect. All Mark had to do was listen to his betters and let the experts handle it. He could have really benefitted from any one of those others performing his play.

So when Karl Shiels and I were cast as The Howie Lee and The Rookie Lee, it became very clear that there was one dominant vision in all of this. Mark had made clear from the start who he wanted and no amount of better advice was going to steer him from that path. The more experienced someone is the less likely they are to try and control everything and it's a credit to Bradwell and his producer Deborah Aydon that Mark got his men in the end. A lesser team would have cast better people and would have run the risk of losing the trust and respect of their most valuable asset: the writer.

Rehearsals began in January 1999 in a miserably cold, wet Shepherd's Bush. Put in digs in a house in Acton town, a short tube ride from The Bush, we got our breakfast but were confined to our rooms at all other times. For every Irish person who has moved to London, there are at least ten more who have conjured up an image in their mind of a damp, unfriendly city, slathered in unceasing tones of grey, and decided to stay away: that was the city we came to. Having nowhere to go after rehearsals, we used to spend our money on pints in the pub under the theatre and try to keep enough for a KFC Zinger Burger before riding home on the train and crashing until it was time to rehearse the next day.

Mike had coined the phrase 'Stand-Up Theatre' for Mark's monologue play and he wanted to see that idea through in rehearsals. Mike recognized the most important aspect of the play was the playing of it; that as a monologue it was not a relaying of events that had happened in the past but a relaying of events in the present tense, *as they happened*. As we told the story, as the audience heard it for the very first time, so we were hearing it for the first time too. Every shock to the audience needed to be a shock to us. This was what Mike meant by 'Stand-Up Theatre'. He didn't want it to be a mere recital of a brilliant play; he wanted to it to be an event.

With language so rich and potentially difficult for a foreign English ear, we also needed a way of fooling people into thinking that we weren't really actors, while being technically proficient enough to keep them on board. Companies like the Royal Shakespeare Company and The Globe have devised tools to help the actor convey Shakespeare clearly and effectively. Mark's language presented a similar challenge and we had to construct a new set of tools; a new way into a new language.

One of the first things we did in the rehearsal room was to list all the characters of the play and turn them into people we both knew, so that when either of us spoke of characters like The Peaches or Ginger Boy, we envisaged the same people, the same tone of voice, the same tics. Karl and I didn't know each other too well but had both been knocking around the Dublin theatre scene for a while so in large part the people we both knew were from this pool. It made sense at the time to use them to put flesh on the bones of characters like the terrifying Avalanche and Ladyboy, though we were good enough never to fess up to the individuals involved.

Early on, Mike had us rehearsing separately, with each of us taking either a morning or an afternoon session, and it engendered a sense of competition between us. I certainly exaggerated how far ahead I was with learning lines and how well it was going.

We both spent weeks in that dark little theatre, with two faces peering at us through the gloom. Mike would sit quite close and Mark would be a few rows back. He was at every rehearsal without fail. Again, he was the dominant force in the room. Whereas Mike allowed me to find a physicality for The Howie that was all my own, I could sense Mark straining his ear for the right rhythm in the language, the proper cadence of each sentence. We had a printed-off script that we worked from and Mark would often stop me mid-sentence to draw my attention to a word and the fact that it was italicized, meaning that word had to be stressed. *Had* to be. *No* question. It was maddening, but years later I would experience the same thing when watching my daughters at Sports Day; the over-protectiveness and the blatant desire for them to succeed.

Doubly maddening was the fact that Mark was always right. I soon learnt that Mark never dealt with the notion of the 'second draft.' What you got was what he had worked on until he was satisfied.

The room was not without its tensions. Mike was an old-hand at dealing with new and emerging writers but I think even he was taken aback by Mark's insistence on sticking to the script to the nth degree. He started calling Mark 'Specky Beckett', after that other guy whose scripts you can't mess with. Mark took it for a while, but eventually it came to a head when he said to Mike 'how about I refer to you as Fat Fuck?' Mike stopped then.

I don't remember much about the opening few shows. Performing a monologue for the first time in front of a (to us) foreign crowd, with a piece as complicated as *Howie*, there was a sickening white heat of adrenaline that ravaged all the synapses in my brain. During the previews, a couple of lines were added to the very end of the play to make things clearer. When we opened, the reviews were very good, and the audience seemed to like it a lot. I think even our landlady came to see it, but if she liked it, it didn't translate into letting us use the kitchen at night. We would have missed our Zinger burgers too much at that stage anyway.

But what was clear early on was that Mark was the star of the show. Most reviews began with a variation on how tired British reviewers were of monologues and Irish theatre in general, but here was something new, something fresh. Which was all bullshit, of course. *Howie* didn't owe anything to those other Irish plays that were around at the time. It was making its own wave.

After the first few weeks, Mark went back to Dublin and we finished our run in London to good houses and then moved to The Civic Theatre in Tallaght, which was Mark's home town. Luckily he knew from early on in rehearsals that we were going there, so many character names had been changed to protect the living and the dead. We were the inaugural show at the theatre, which was opened in March 1999, and had to contend with many teething problems. The main one was that after the opening night, we went from a full house to an audience of about 20 people a night, due to the fact that not many people knew that the theatre existed and those who did couldn't find it. The Civic has since grown to be a big part of the community and I'm proud to have helped cut that ribbon with such a fine show, especially because Mark was 'the local-guy-turned-writer.'

After that, we moved into Dublin city centre, to the Andrew's Lane Theatre, before heading to Edinburgh where it all blew away into outer space. The reviews were immense and the queues to get in were around the block. Again, it was the play itself that was the thing. It had somehow managed to excite people with nothing more than language: the power of its images. I remember we had a blind guy in the front row one night at The Assembly Rooms, who, when The Rookie describes The Howie's body being ripped asunder, put his hands over his eyes to try and stop himself seeing it.

With its excess of bodily fluids and sexual functions, its comments on women, race, the mentally disabled and homosexuality, the play said a lot about the thoughts that ran through the heads of these two young men. It managed to offend everyone in equal measure, which surely is the fairest way of causing offense, and we had our share of walk outs and stinky reviews based on how disgusted some critic was. Everyone could find a reason not to like the play, and every town or city we played in had its own preference for what it conceived as funny or not; for all its allusions to myth, Kung Fu and Cowboy movies, it was still damn funny. Dublin recognized the humour but the middle-class theatre-going audience had preconceived notions of the working-class characters and we had a harder time winning them over than most other places. In Plymouth they never made a sound; I still don't quite know what happened there. Glasgow had the keenest understanding of the humour and it was there, I believe, that the play found its spiritual home. London, Edinburgh and New York had an intellectually curious crowd, who were used to seeing new work in the grungy, edgy venues we played in, so they were open minded and receptive to the ideas and the strange language. San Francisco was slightly lost for words, and we suffered badly there due to their ticketing policy. A new Sam Shepard play, directed by the man himself and starring a clutch of film stars, had played before us, and The Magic Theatre, who were producing, came up with the ingenious plan of selling the best seats in the house if they bought tickets to the following two plays as well, one of which was *Howie*. We were assured we were sold out before we arrived but we actually played to half-empty houses. To make things worse, there were people queuing around the block trying to get a ticket and being told it was impossible to sell a seat that had already been sold, even though no-one bothered to show up and fill it.

But things changed immeasurably when we reached New York. The *New York Times*' critic Ben Brantley, the man they said could (and still can) make or break a show, had written a review that was a love-letter to Mark, and that guaranteed us maximum success in a city where success means everything, where everyone wants to get close to you because maybe some of that success will rub off on them too. Mark was with us for much of our stay and was the toast of the town. We were hamstrung by American Equity, the actors' union, on the size of the house we could play, and the exclusivity made the show even more in demand. Everybody was trying to get into the tiny venue at PS122 on the Lower East Side and everyone who hadn't snapped up a ticket in the first few days after the brilliant reviews started rolling off the presses could get lost. Stories were filtering through to the dressing room of celebrities being turned away at the door, terribly upset, not because the theatre staff didn't know who they were, but because the theatre staff knew exactly who they were and still turned them away, and they had to watch the great unwashed file past them with their tickets in their hands and smug grins on their faces.

For the three Dublin lads involved it was a rite of passage. In your home town you're cut down to size at every available opportunity: someone always remembers you running around in nappies when you were only a baby. In London, we struggled against the usual stereotyping and that awful old boys' club snobbery that runs through British theatre. But in America we arrived fully formed. We knew how good we were and now everyone else did too. The big guns got involved. A deal was struck with Broadway producers to take the show to the next level. Contracts were negotiated and deals put in place. All we now had to do was finish the New York and San Francisco runs, hold off for six months and then come back and conquer The Big Apple again. Simple.

And then it all fell apart.

With about two weeks to go, American Equity stepped in and brought the whole thing to a halt. As I said earlier, one of the stipulations with us being there was that we played small venues. The Magic Theatre, for whatever reason, put us in a bigger venue than what suited the union. So when it came to green-lighting our permits, Equity said there was no reason two American actors couldn't play the parts, which is a nice way of telling you to put your frock back in the closet and let the air out of the tyres on your carriage, because you're not coming to the ball.

I think it must have been written in the stars that the show was never going to play New York again. Even if we had managed to get past the union, we were scheduled to open at The Minetta Lane Theatre in Greenwich Village, less than two miles from the World Trade Centre, on September 10th 2001.

In 2006 Fiach Mac Conghail, director of The Abbey Theatre and a big fan of Mark's work, put the play on again in The Peacock, directed by Jimmy Fay, with Karl and me reprising our roles. I was afraid that the two-week rehearsal period wouldn't be enough, but within days I remembered every line. I was also fully aware that the play had never left me. I had carried it into everything I had done since, so deeply was it carved into my psyche. Those rhythms, those thoughts, that aggression. It was both a blessing and a curse.

Karl and I were both stretching it a bit as believable young lads, though to a certain extent the fact that we were older and still thought like guys in their early to mid-twenties added a sadness to their plight as disenfranchised men, less concerned with having jobs and raising families than with seeking revenge for scabies-infested mattresses. Mark thought about changing bits of the play to accommodate our ages but in the end left it as was. As an actor I was far more experienced now and gave a much more technically polished performance, but I can't help thinking that I had lost a certain fire in my belly; an anger that I had as a young man. The show was so much more accomplished but much less raw, and as a result it was not the explosive force that had battered Dublin, London, and New York five years before.

At the time of writing, Mark has staged a new version of the play with the wonderful Tom Vaughan Lawlor playing both roles. Half of me is dying to go; to see it all played out in my mind again, to meet those characters and revisit the events that lead up to that most epic of tragic endings. The other part of me has kept away, not wanting to admit that it has outlived the actors who felt such a part of it. I have no doubt that *Howie the Rookie* will prove to be a truly great play, outliving the small guy with the glasses who wrote it too.

5| Crestfall: A Production Study

Sara Keating

Mark O'Rowe's first monologue play for women was produced at the Gate Theatre in 2003. Despite critical acclaim, the play proved to be enormously controversial and performances were regularly punctuated by audience walk-outs. When O'Rowe's first collected plays were published by Nick Hern Books in 2011, he re-wrote the text. This production study aims to capture the various different elements of the original production from the perspective of those involved, to give a rounded view of what it was that an audience found so challenging about the work in its premiere production.

Mark O'Rowe, Writer

Crestfall was an incredibly tough play to write. A word-a-day type of thing. I was determined that it would just be about women, because that was something I hadn't done before, and also that it would be the darkest thing I had ever written. I was pretty vulnerable about my writing at this time. I wrote it after finishing a commission from the Abbey that they didn't want to produce, and it was a protective kind of thing. It wasn't conscious, but I think there was something about showing off how low I could go. I suppose I wanted people to hate it, to push people away. If I wanted you to hate it and you did, well that's not failure.

The first person I gave *Crestfall* to when I was finished was my agent. He passed it on to the director Rufus Norris, who read it and wanted to do it. He did a sort of rehearsed reading in London and invited a load of different companies to come but no-one bit. Then Michael Colgan read it and loved it, and wanted to do it with Garry

Hynes. I was flattered, but when I met with Michael he said he didn't know if it was right for the Gate, that maybe we should do it at the Project Arts Centre instead. He was smart enough to predict how the audience would react. It just confirmed all my insecurities about the play and I went on the defensive, and said no: it had to be put on at the Gate. I wasn't aware how specific an audience it was. They would put up with the odd Pinter or Beckett but only if you gave them what they wanted the rest of the time.

My memory of rehearsals is quite faint, though I was there every day. Even though it means taking a month off work, it is really important for the writer to be in the room. You have to protect your own work: you would be stupid not to. What I do remember is how respectful everyone was of the text. But when I read it later [when putting together his work in a collected edition] it didn't feel authentic, and I could see why the audience wouldn't get behind it. It was mean-spirited, vacant, the least poetic or most boiled down of anything I had written.

I started rewriting it while I was in the middle of rehearsing *Terminus*. I did the rewrites on a printed out copy while walking into town for rehearsal over 3 weeks, and I think that naturally influenced some of the changes I made to the play. It wasn't just a case of humanizing it, making it nicer. It was too jagged, dissonant, it didn't flow properly. I didn't actually change anything about the plot, except for one small detail, the bit with Olive and the dog. That was one of the parts that the audience was most offended by, but that actually wasn't why I cut it. There was a flaw in the logic of it, plot-wise: the dog couldn't have been in that scene.

It was hard to watch the play when people were walking out every few minutes. I remember after the show people coming up to me and saying 'did you write this play? It is the worst thing I have ever seen.' It was mostly women. I don't know if that's because they found it more offensive or that they weren't shy about telling me what they thought. At the start, I thought, 'fuck them.' I was deliberately being provocative. But it was actually heart-breaking.

Garry Hynes, Director

I was always a fan of Mark's work and thought he was a tremendous writer for the theatre, so when I first read *Crestfall* there was no question that I wouldn't direct it. I was challenged by it, yes, but I knew I wanted the challenge. His gift for language is extraordinary and he has a vision which I think is unique. In terms of his lyrical voice, you could see it as part of a continuum in Irish theatre, but it's a strange bend in the road.

Although you can't deny the form, to characterize the plays as monologue gives a false impression that there is only one voice and one perspective on the story. *Crestfall* is really an epic play and you get a huge landscape mapped out in front of you and an extraordinary multiplicity of perspectives on the story. The biggest challenge is that you are taking three actors and putting them on, in sequence, alone, asking them to tell that story so an audience can experience their world and see the landscape of the play without the usual signifiers of what I would call faux-naturalism. Actually, if you are going to compare a monologue play to what we call realist or naturalist play you are setting up false conflict; no act of theatre is naturalist. Theatre is an act where one person commits to watching another person on stage; that's theatre. And with a monologue play, it is still an act of artifice even if the actor is speaking directly to the audience. They are speaking from an imagined world.

There were big design challenges for myself and Francis O'Connor too, and there were no easy answers. We used mirrors to design an environment that reflected how the characters felt, what the world looked like to them in their imagination. We certainly had no intention of showing any of the backstreets of the town or anything. It was more imaginative. But in rehearsals we worked a lot with a town plan, which Aisling O'Sullivan, who played Olive Day, had drawn. *Crestfall* is about three people and a series of events they all share, so we wanted a common sense of where they were. Like when the characters mentioned the river, I wanted the actors and myself to be in the same place in our heads. We also rehearsed together a lot of the time. Even though they performed their monologues separately, I would deliberately make the call so that we were working with at least two of the actors together: you can't tell the details of the story without being absolutely clear about it.

Crestfall is about family relationships, even if it isn't the traditional family, but the content was challenging. The images of violence and sex it conjures up are brutal. I didn't find it misogynistic [as some reviews suggested]. I wouldn't have done it if I did. But it was challenging for my position as *loco parentis* for an audience too and the ideas proved a step too far for the usual Gate audience. But why would I do that play if I wanted to soften the blow for them? It is the play's ability to create these savage images that is part of its power.

I doubt there was a performance where we ended with the same audience that we started with. A lot of the audience were quite shocked by it and either left – 'I don't want to have this kind of experience' – or expressed their protest by staying away. There were a couple of times where people would be muttering leaving, but there were no big incidents. We were concerned that we weren't getting the audience, as you always would be. The context you create for a production is so important, especially when you are dealing with new work, and maybe that was [part of the problem]. You can't switch on an audience for a new play like that; you can't give them Jane Austen and then *Crestfall* and expect them to have a coherent experience. But I was and still am passionate about the play. I am just sorry that audiences were walking out, but it didn't affect my attitude to the decisions I made.

Francis O'Connor, Designer

I had worked on monologue plays before *Crestfall*. I had designed Conor McPherson's *This Lime Tree Bower* [in 1999], but *Crestfall* was something different. When I first read it, I just loved the dark, rich language of the play. The first challenge I had to consider as a designer was how I could help sustain one person speaking on stage without overwhelming the words. I really wanted to do it and it remains one of the things I am most proud of.

At the start I had to really fight the impulse to add things in terms of staging. Usually as a designer you need to be responsible to text and stage and directions. You are concerned with the mechanics of what you need to make a play work. The most important thing was not to make it literal; I wanted to create a synthesis of the women and the words. Because the play was actually very specific in its description of location, I didn't feel obliged to provide anything concrete. What I came up with instead was a sort of disjointed abstraction. I had this idea of playing with a mirror effect, and I created a frame of three panels of shattered mirror, one of which floated above the actors at an angle. The effect was to reflect the actors, but in a way that you could never see the actor's entire body at any one time. I thought that reflected the disjointed lives of these women. It gave the play a weird sense of location, even though it was a non-naturalistic one. It is a hard bleak ugly world, with not a chink of light in it, but it still has a strange beauty.

We had a lot of discussion about the costuming of the different characters, which we wanted to be different from each other but complementary. But I knew immediately after first reading the play that I wanted to contrast blackness with flesh. I decided to use all black outfits against bare skin, with each woman revealing more flesh than the next one: Marie was the most covered, Eileen was the most exposed,

Aisling was wearing a really short dress and very high heels. This meant we were very conscious of their gestures. I remember the figures in the model box: they seemed all bare arms and limbs. It was Francis Bacon-ish. It made it look like they had been butchered.

The image of water is really important in the play and I had this idea of using the floor to play with that. There is a scene where Tilly, who was played by Eileen Walsh, describes finding a child's toy in the gutter, and there was a moment when she reached into the floor and picked it out of a pool of water. Until that moment the characters had all moved about the stage freely and for the audience it looked like a hard surface. Suddenly it looked like she was dipping her hand into the floor and it really elevated the whole scene, made you think how connected the world and the characters were.

Working with the lighting designer Rupert Murray, we ensured the stage was entirely side-lit. We used ballet masking at the side so that he could get the light across the stage but you couldn't see where the light-source was or where the light ended. This made the actors' bodies seem like they were separate from the landscape, or like they were illuminated from within, like figures floating in space. With a play like *Crestfall* the actors don't need a literal world. They need to be liberated, and the direct dialogue with the audience, the monologue form, made it possible to do that.

Eileen Walsh, Tilly McQuarrie

The first time I saw any of Mark's work was when they did *Howie the Rookie* in the Bush and I thought: 'if only they were female characters.' I don't remember how I was first approached to be in *Crestfall*, but I do remember being in the room on the first day of rehearsals and I was petrified, but Mark's writing is so overwhelmingly attractive it quashed any fears I had of Garry Hynes as a director and it made me want to be brave. It was the poetry, the beauty of something that was also so violent, that struck me. I felt very lucky to have the opportunity to explore a territory I had never even dreamt of.

I'm aware that people feel Mark's writing for women is suspect, but people always have opinions about strong female roles. Male characters can be violent and aggressive towards women, and people don't say anything, and in *Crestfall* the female characters had a chance to show that too. The thing is no-one escapes in Mark's plays. The men are deranged and sex-fuelled and violent and thankfully the women are too; too often women are left to decorate the stage and service the male characters. So when the chance came for *Crestfall* I felt lucky to be involved with it.

Crestfall wasn't the first time I had done a monologue play. I had done *Disco Pigs* in 1996, but that was different as I wasn't on stage on my own and I had Cillian [Murphy]'s energy to feed off. The thing about *Crestfall* is that we were each on stage on our own; there's no-one to save you then. I was an absolute shambling wreck before I went on, completely petrified. But the action and the words come so fast that the audience is too caught up in what happens next to notice if you make a mistake or if they do they forgive you quickly. You have to remember that, but it is hard. One trick I use is to learn the play in my own words as well – even if it's dialogue or Shakespeare – so I can save myself if I need to.

I know that some people remember the play as being disgusting or disturbing, but for me it was always a thrill, more than anything else. It was even more dangerous to be performing it in a theatre like the Gate. I think that with any of Mark's stuff, you are always aware that there will probably be a level of upset for the audience but if the theatre is brave enough to put it on you feel more protected. Still nothing prepares you for standing on stage and the audience tutting or walking out, and the Gate is so intimate you could hear people making excuses to their partners, or whoever, as they left.

In rehearsals though, sometimes I thought maybe we weren't going far enough. I remember chatting with Garry about the set and the costume for my character, Tilly. I had my own ideas about the costume. Because the set was mirrored, I thought, maybe Tilly should be naked from waist down or wearing red pants underneath her dress, so as you walked on so you would see them reflected. I kept seeing the world in my head like a film, and those ideas were probably more like scenes from a film than a play, or what the audience would imagine when they were watching. Anyway, Garry wasn't keen on my idea. When you are working on a monologue play, it is especially intense because it is very much about the one on one relationship between you and the director. You are sharing personal things to open up the work and there is a huge amount of trust in it. Anyway, we wore different black dresses instead.

The set was a black box too, made of mirrors, so everything inside was reflected back into it. When you walked on it was just pitch darkness and it was really hard to find your spot. When you looked back, you were talking to yourself in this black mirror. It felt like very uncertain ground. But there was this part at the end of my monologue where I reached into the ground to get a toy and my hand came out dripping wet: I would bend and dip my hand into pool of water, which was the only thing on the entire set, but the audience would never see it. It was a revelation.

For me, Mark writes about the little dark corners of all of our minds that we choose to ignore to pretend to be civilized. He demands actors to be both fragile and aggressive and allows us to explore these often-ignored emotions. Mark was very open about discussing the work and its origins, but those stories are for the rehearsal room. The rehearsal room is a private space and once you let people in it becomes a performance rather than a discovery.

Playing Tilly, I felt a real affinity with her. I might not ever have had to give a dog a wank like she did but Mark's writing for me is about the way we suppress our aggression and refuse to talk about terrible human behaviour. Ultimately it is about surviving and reaching beyond to break the surface of the water.

Aisling O'Sullivan, Olive Day

I was excited when I read *Crestfall* because it was the first time I was being given the opportunity to command a theatre fully on my own. It would just be myself and the audience for twenty minutes, and I was excited about being trusted with their attention. Usually when you are working, there are other people – actors, sets and costumes – involved. But with *Crestfall* it was just language and your performance that had to do everything. I had to conjure up a community out of thin air.

Usually when you are rehearsing, you learn your lines, of course, but a lot of it comes naturally over the course of a four-week rehearsal and through your interactions with the other actors. With *Crestfall* I had to sit down and just study the script, learn my lines, like the performance at the end was an exam. I had an intense fear every night when I went on stage that I would not know where the words were.

I would get very nervous about 20 minutes before I went on, and I would speed recite my lines to myself, to make sure that I hadn't forgotten them. But there was no room for fear once you walked on stage because you were concentrating so much on the language. The language was so rhythmic that it fused with your body. It wasn't even like music. It was like dance. It wasn't enough to say 'I'm walking', you had to strut your stuff. My costume was very provocative too. I had these really high heels, which made me feel like I was on stilts, bigger than life. It was so brazen and I think that helped me. I wouldn't be confident like that at all.

There were no real pauses for me as I delivered [the monologue] because Olive was a character who didn't have any self-reflection. She wasn't a 'device'. She wasn't thinking about what happened. She was describing it just as it happened. That was what I liked about her. She was a very honest character. There was no attempt to charm you or dazzle you with charisma. Her disgust was honest. Her enjoyment of other people's suffering was honest.

Even though we were on stage on our own, there was a dramatic coherence between the three characters. Sex, I suppose. We rehearsed together a good bit and that helped, as it was very useful for us to see how the others were approaching the material. Even though we were never on stage together, it was a very symbiotic experience. I remember the big breakthrough for me came when I was watching Eileen one day. She looked like a person trapped in a nightmare, vividly recreating a dream. That really shifted things and opened the play up for me.

Garry is very specific as a director and asked us to bring in things to rehearsals – photographs of what we thought the characters described in the play looked like and that – and that helped all of us to feel grounded, like there was a real community that our characters belonged to. I drew a map as part of that exercise, and it was very much a rural town. Mark and Garry were keen to veer away from the Dublin concept, but it was recognizable in the way Dublin was at the time. Pockets of roughness and I think that's what the audience reacted against.

It never occurred to me that the content of the play might be offensive. It was a very unreal world that we were creating, a poetic world, and it never struck me that people would get so het up about it. It was pretty naïve, but I just hadn't considered that people might not be able to digest it. As the run went on we got to know which passages would be marked by the sound of seats swinging up. The thing was not to let it disrupt your concentration.

But in a way I actually applaud the people who walked out. Disgust is a powerful emotion. They felt strongly enough that they were prepared to take a stand. There would be questions afterwards. People would come up to you in the bar, wanting to know how we felt about being in it. At the same time, it was equally valid to stay and see the denouement.

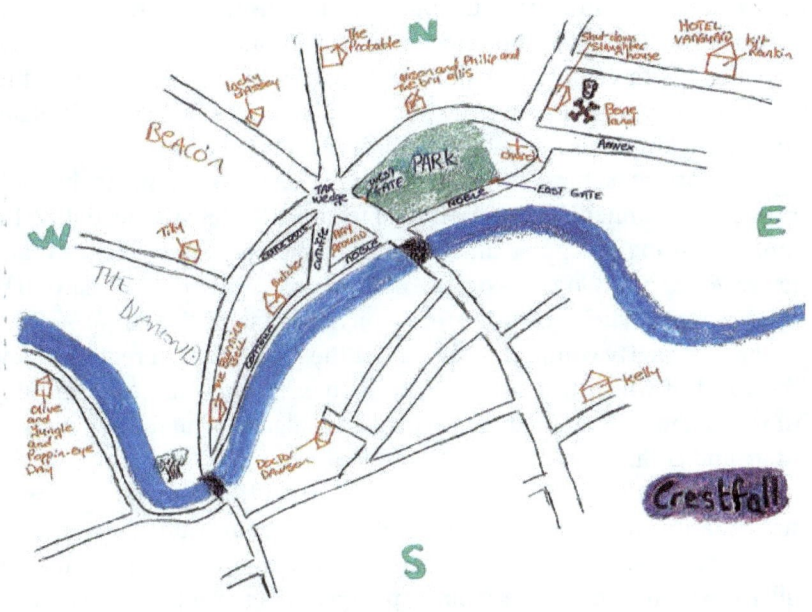

Drawing by Aisling O'Sullivan, for rehearsals for the 2003 production of *Crestfall* at The Gate Theatre

Crestfall Review by Fintan O'Toole

The Irish Times, May 22nd 2003

Those of us whose childhoods unfolded in the era before boredom was outlawed may remember the phrase: 'Tell us a picture.' When all conversation had dried up and all activities had been exhausted, you recounted, with your own elisions and exaggerations, the story of a film you'd seen. I'm not sure if Mark O'Rowe remembers the same injunction, but in his new play he tells us a picture.

Not a pretty picture, either. If *Crestfall* was indeed a movie, it would probably be banned. The story it tells features brutal sex, bestiality, the public torturing of a horse and a climax of such extreme violence that it makes *Reservoir Dogs* seem like a Hallmark Mother's Day card. The three women who recount it are a nymphomaniac, a whore and a mother – a pretty comprehensive set of the old female stereotypes. And the world in which it is set is a 'savage quarter' halfway between Mad Max and the Irish midlands, a surreal amalgam of nameless housing estate and gothic post-apocalyptic landscape.

Yet *Crestfall* is also a highly sophisticated and serious piece of theatre and, in Garry Hynes's electrifying production, a completely convincing one. The three narrators who occupy the stage in turn and tell a single story from overlapping perspectives may operate like movie cameras taking shots from different angles. In their narratives they 'scope' and 'click', moving from wide shots to close-ups. But the piece is nevertheless quintessentially theatrical. It hovers on the borderline between showing and telling in a way that is utterly dependent on the dangerous live presence of three superb actors.

What makes *Crestfall* such an important escape from the monologue form that has become such a cliché in contemporary Irish theatre, indeed, is O'Rowe's theatrical exploration of a world that is drenched in cinematic imagery. Within a short 70 minutes and the apparently simple form of a three-handed narrative, he is actually weaving in and out of four different ways of telling a story: cinema, short story, theatrical performance and epic poetry.

The most obvious parallels are with the late Beckett plays and with the social surrealism of Jim Cartwright's *Road*. But, although these influences are undoubtedly present, *Crestfall*, for all its lurid details and occasionally foul language, is actually rather close in form and intent to *The Playboy of the Western World*. A line in that play, Pegeen's remark that 'there's a great gap between a gallous story and a dirty deed' is also the best summary of *Crestfall*. The play is not about squalor and violence, it's about the great gap between the reality of human degradation and the heroic glamour that representations of brutality acquire in our culture.

To enter this gap safely, O'Rowe puts on the armour that has served writers so well throughout theatrical history: stylized, poetic language. His text is hypnotically rhythmic, and highly artificial, using a language wrenched from its colloquial roots, but still clear and concise enough to bear the narrative weight. This is utterly crucial to the distancing effect that he requires. It makes *Crestfall* no more, nor no less, violent than, say, *Medea*. The vicious story is held in constant tension with the cool, rigorous form.

No less crucial, though, is the tone of the production. The tension between showing and telling demands an absolute clarity of purpose from the actors. They need to embody enough of the action to make the play live as a piece of theatre, but not so much as to tip the balance into vulgar bathos. And under Garry Hynes's remarkably supple direction, Aisling O'Sullivan, Marie Mullen and Eileen Walsh do so magnificently.

The ground is laid by the brilliantly integrated interaction of Francis O'Connor's unsettling hall-of-mirrors set, Rupert Murray's lighting and Paul Arditti's creepy sound design, all of which combine to create a bubble of time and place. It has its own reality that is never literal, but is nonetheless unsettling.

Within this eerie space, the passion of the narrators tells us that the story is true, but the surroundings deny us the comfort of verifying that this is so. There are no external reference points, just the voices and movements of the actors. And all three occupy the space with startling conviction, even as they enter it from very different angles. O'Sullivan is full of a feline yearning that carries an undertone of threat, Mullen warm but wary, Walsh vulnerable, but with the indefatigability of a survivor.

Between them, they exert an unbreakable hold. What is essentially a highly complex exercise in form gains a ferocious immediacy. *Crestfall* becomes deeply shocking, not for the lurid content of the story, but for the insidious mastery with which that story overcomes our repulsion and acquires an epic, almost mythic status. Which is precisely what this brave and accomplished play wants to do to us, raising as it does so some urgent questions about our culture.

Audience Crestfallen by Rachel Andrews
The Sunday Tribune

Oh what a tricky creature drama is. Here is a production with all the elements in place. It has a superb cast, an award-winning director, a designer gifted with a wealth of creative resources and a script, which blisters its way across the pages, the writing lush, delicate, poised. And yet, it comes up short.

The problem, it seems, is in the translation of the script from page to stage. To read Mark O'Rowe's tale of three women locked in a dark, desperate place where brutal sex is the only trade most people know, animal cruelty is the order of the day and where kindness is an aberration is to hold your breath and follow the writer on a terrible, inevitably tragic journey. To soak up his prose, highly stylized and poetic, is to be in awe of his talents as a writer.

And yet, somehow, on stage, this is lost. Although O'Rowe has constructed a terrible but complete narrative in *Crestfall*, the writing of the story is as important as the events on the stage. His creation of a surreal, savage underworld, set somewhere in Ireland's midlands, needs surreal, otherworldly language, recognizable but difficult, stripped as it is of accents or specifics and pared down to the very bone. His characters have their own, artificial way of speaking. They 'click', they 'scope', they 'behold'. They speak, almost in verse, unrhyming poetry in short, staccato sentences.

On paper, this is great stuff. And if the short sentences are confusing then, you can go back, reread, and find the threads you might have lost. On stage, there is no time for that. Instead, one is asked to give immense concentration to what is being said, in order to figure out where the story is going. It is a lot to ask.

O'Rowe has chosen the rather trendy monologue form to tell his story. The women arrive onto stage separately, one appearing as the other disappears, to tell their tales. There is Olive Day, the sex addict, whose marriage to a man she doesn't respect only fuels her desires. There is Alison Ellis, a mother struggling to keep her marriage alive despite a wandering husband and a disfigured child. Finally, there is Tilly McQuarrie, local whore and heroin addict. There is a narrative thread holding these stories together, but it is not clear on the stage. Effectively, each woman is telling the same story from a different perspective, but after each monologue, the audience claps – it is as if we have finality where there should be none.

In all other ways, though, this is a superbly crafted production. Garry Hynes direction is sparse and entirely focused. She dresses the women in black, tightly choreographs their movements and uses minimal props. In fact, the only moment where the set is used – when Tilly dips her hand into a puddle – is wonderfully effective for its very uniqueness. Aisling O'Sullivan, Marie Mullen and Eileen Walsh are tremendous as the three different, troubled women while Francis O'Connor's set of mirrors and lights creates perfectly the claustrophobic, threatening atmosphere. However, even these cannot compensate for the basic difficulty the drama presents – the lack of a discernible story. But you know, it almost works, and although the risks taken by O'Rowe didn't quite pay off this time, his talent as a writer is confirmed. His theatrical talents must now follow suit.[7]

---

[7] For more critical perspectives see Luke Clancy's review in *The Times* (London), 23 May 2003 and Karen Fricker's in *The Guardian*, 24 May 2003.

6 | Performativity and Class in Mark O'Rowe's Monologue Plays

Tim Barrett

Mark O'Rowe's *Anna's Ankle* (1997), *Howie the Rookie* (1999), *Crestfall* (2003) and *Terminus* (2007) collectively form one of the recent chapters in a distinguished genealogy of monologue plays in Irish theatre. O'Rowe uses the monologue form to create worlds marked by violence and abjection, producing narratives of despair and depravity occasionally uplifted through moments of redemption. In this chapter, I will be applying theories of performativity posited by J.L. Austin and Judith Butler to O'Rowe's monologue plays to uncover their theatrical operations and to consider how they may be received by middle-class audiences.

J.L. Austin put forward the theory that 'performative utterances' (utterances that perform actions) do not simply describe a state of affairs, but bring a state of affairs into being. He uses the examples of, *inter alia*, the utterance of the words 'I do' at the marriage ceremony (bringing the marriage into existence), the naming of a ship, the swearing of an oath, and the making of a bet. Austin theorizes the issuing of utterances as the performance of a locutionary act ('roughly equivalent to uttering a certain sentence with a certain sense and reference'), containing within it an illocutionary act ('such as informing, ordering, warning, undertaking'), with the possibility of also performing a perlocutionary act ('such as convincing, persuading, deterring') (Austin 109). Illocutionary force is the effect of an illocutionary act, whilst a perlocutionary effect is the consequence of the illocutionary act, which may or may not be the intended effect of the illocutionary act. In this process, Austin uses the term 'uptake' to describe the addressee's comprehension of what is being communicated to them and the nature of that comprehension. He creates the category of 'infelicities' to include the 'doctrine of *the things that can be and go wrong* on the occasion of such utterances' and which in some way prevent the proper functioning of the performative utterance (e.g. in a marriage ceremony, if the groom is already married, this will render void the performative utterance of the words 'I do') (14).

The monologues performed by O'Rowe's characters do not simply describe fictional worlds, they carry the illocutionary force of informing and representing, and a variety of perlocutionary consequences that may include persuading, entertaining, shocking, amusing, offending, and so on. My aim is to examine O'Rowe's illocutionary strategies in his monologue plays and refer to their possible perlocutionary consequences. The title of J.L. Austin's seminal book *How to do Things with Words* (1962) prompts the question of what O'Rowe is doing with *his* words. Susan Bennett, however, cautions that 'textual analyses can provide interesting and useful explications of strategies available for audience interpretation. But however detailed, these analyses can only represent a small part of the interactive relations that constitute the nexus of the two receptive frames'[8] (Bennett 161). In the absence of detailed empirical studies of audiences' reception of plays (e.g. the use of questionnaires following the performance), my consideration of perlocutionary effects will necessarily be mindful of the limitations Bennett refers to.

Patrick Lonergan, writing of recent Irish monologue plays, including O'Rowe's, has observed that 'there is certainly a class divide between the middle-class audiences before whom most of these plays were premiered and the mostly working-class characters that populate the stage' (Lonergan 184). The class divide to which Lonergan refers will provide a site for criticism of O'Rowe's monologue plays. Austin attributes language with the power to bring into being that to which it refers. When O'Rowe's characters construct worlds through language, they also constitute spectators as onlookers within those worlds. The spectators' need to imagine the narrated worlds in order to comprehend the action draws them intimately into the theatre-making process. I will attempt to show how the illocutionary force of the monologues shapes middle-class encounters with represented worlds of brutality and abjection.

---

[8] The two receptive frames are the inner frame, demarcating the playing space, and the outer frame, embracing both audience and performers.

Anna's Ankle was first performed on 17 February, 1997 as part of Bedrock Theatre Company's *Electroshock: A Theatre of Cruelty Season*. It features an unnamed snuff video director who, during a break from filming a video, narrates a monologue describing his relationship with Anna, a young painter from Ennis who has travelled to Dublin to find work. *Anna's Ankle* could be described as a monologue play which frames the narrative of a snuff video, also entitled *Anna's Ankle*. The two are conflated from the outset when the stage directions indicate that the narrator 'shows us the front page – it says 'Anna's Ankle" before the narrator utters 'Anna's Ankle' and proceeds with his monologue ('Unpublished Script' 2). In saying these words, he is bringing into being both the monologue play and the half-filmed snuff video to which it refers. The narrator's technique as snuff video director and as a monologist appears to be indistinguishable. Throughout the monologue, he envisions the subject of his planned video, Anna, and in particular fetishizes her 'dark tanned ankles and white canvas shoes. The contrast, you know? Canvas and skin. Light and dark. Rough and smooth. Superb. I'm thinking to myself, she'll wear those shoes in the film, or something white anyway. The contrast will fuel the fetish' (2).

The narrator's imaginative process is instrumental in selecting suitable actors for his videos and visualizing scenes in which they will appear. And if the narrator is 'always imagining, creating shots' (3), the spectators are creating reciprocal shots, and thereby being drawn in to his image-making venture. The director produces the snuff videos based on his imagined scenarios and in turn compels spectators to imaginatively produce it for themselves: no other camera angle is available other than the narrator's. It could be argued that the narrator's vocabulary of avant-garde cinema is used as an illocutionary act to address a specifically middle-class artistic sensibility. Once addressed and identified as a group in this way, spectators may experience a greater connection and involvement with the narrated action.

Unlike the major part of O'Rowe's other work, the characters in *Anna's Ankle* display middle-class characteristics, albeit in many cases affected. The narrator and Anna discuss and assess her education, her artistic ambitions and what kind of paintings she paints ('good paintings or … that Picasso shite?' (4)). After having sex, Anna complains of his 'misogynistic crudity' after he describes their coupling as 'me fucking you' rather than 'making love' (5). He details the many prescription drugs he will require for the making of the video and their supposed effects on Anna. His own pretensions as an arthouse film director also allude to middle-class aspirations, although infused with irony: 'So I tells her I'm a film maker and would she want to be in an avant-garde piece of cinema. More arthouse than mainstream. She can make a couple of quid off me' (3).

The narrator discusses his art extensively and is keen to distinguish his own contribution to the project from Liam's: 'I'm about artistry, Liam's about technicals, and I think we strike a good balance in our work. We're like the partners. I write the scripts, though. I'm the idea man' (4). After disclosing how he intends to complete his project by filming Liam amputating Anna's feet below the ankles ('The blood flow over them. The contrast between white bone and crimson' (10)), he proclaims that 'the standing up without feet represents her will to live, to stay alive, and that's my theme. The strength of the human spirit. The instinctual need to survive' (11).

The narrator's claims to a status as an art-house film director, bound up with an upwardly mobile class consciousness, may resonate with middle-class audiences, but only accompanied by irony. If O'Rowe's illocutionary intention may be to affront middle-class sensibilities by packaging sadistic violence in middle-class artistic terminology, the perlocutionary effects may not just be, predictably, disgust, revulsion and resistance but also laughter if *Anna's Ankle* is received as black comedy. Whatever the perlocutionary outcome, it may be said that O'Rowe skilfully dissolves the distinction between a monologue play and a snuff video and constitutes spectators as participants in that image-making process. *Anna's Ankle* represents a provocative insight into a disturbed and depraved mind and an invitation to at least face into the most abject social recesses.

Howie the Rookie (1999), O'Rowe's most successful play, features two separate monologues, one delivered by the Howie Lee, one by the Rookie Lee, whose narratives intersect. Brian Singleton comments that 'the narratives do not speak about the other more successful world. Their world is exclusively insular, and thus any action that takes place within it is not at all motivated by opposition or protest against social status, as a middle-class audience might interpret it' (80). The insularity Singleton describes is partly conveyed by the play's lack of recognizable Dublin landmarks, which if offered, could perhaps allow easy access into the narratives. Unlike *Anna's Ankle* and *Terminus*, which contain several references to Dublin street names and other landmarks, there are few identifiable geographical markings, other than Dame Street, where Ollie, Peaches and the Howie Lee alight from the bus. With limited geographical bearings, middle-class spectators may be positioned at a privileged remove, looking down upon a fictional world broadly resembling a disadvantaged suburb of Dublin.

The characters in *Howie the Rookie* speak in a poeticized, compressed urban idiom, often dispensing with personal pronouns and abbreviating wherever possible. Language is a marker of both class and gender and identifies a subordinated social group whose prowess is achieved primarily through acts of sex and violence. As these events are not enacted on stage, language takes over the function of representation – the sex and violence, and the language used to represent them, thus become inseparable.

The callous, casual and functional attitudes to sex evidenced in the behaviour of the Howie and Rookie Lee towards their respective sexual partners Avalanche ('Starts pullin' me off bandy, wringin' me flute. Fuck it, tell the truth, I had her three times and dug it to fuck' (Plays: One 186)) and Bernie ('Lodgy-bodgy hard. Come quick, a post-coital caress, she deserves it, we dress' (208)), as represented through language, point to a societal desensitization to the possibilities of meaningful human warmth and connection. The debasement of sex, materialized through bodily disrespect, is mirrored in the narrated acts of violence:

> Peaches lays in.
> Body shots, head shots, not too hard, have to say, gently bruisin' the handsome cunt's ribs. Split lip, good one, swollen eye swellin' up. The Rookie tries to defend himself. He's feeble. I hold his arms anyway.
>
> . . . .
> Peaches finishes off with a right-left combo to the mush, right hook to the darby. (194)

The compressed language evokes a swift and vigorous physical assault. 'Mush' and 'darby' are slang words for the face and stomach respectively, words whose meanings will be readily comprehensible to certain social groups and spectators, and not to others. A deeper function, for the narrator, may be to morally distance himself from the violence by safely packaging it in slang, which is always removed from standard, formal language. The linguistic displacement of violence is echoed by the Howie's own ambivalence towards the attack ('Not really into it. Must be all that runnin', me stomach's queasy' (194)). If the Howie's strategy of distancing himself from the violence through language is necessary for him to live in a world where violence is a respected currency, middle-class spectators may also on some level be insulated from the narrated violence either through a lack of comprehension or identification with that language. The language employed by the Howie and Rookie Lee is used as a badge of membership of a specific social group and to distinguish those who are outsiders to that group. Unlike much of the language of *Anna's Ankle* and *Terminus*, the speech patterns of the Lees do not conform to educated middle-class speech conventions. Their monologues (speech acts) may therefore have the illocutionary force of situating middle-class spectators as voyeurs of their world, offering only a limited access and engagement with it.

The pursuit and assault of the Rookie Lee in Part One, and the fight with Bernie's son in Part Two form violent preludes to the centrepiece of the play, the duel between the Rookie Lee and Ladyboy. The two circle one another, skirmish and part, before abandoning all stances and inhibitions:

> Jabs an' uppercuts, feints an' parries are abandoned as useless, traded for tearin' an' pummellin' an' cuts an' eye flaps hangin' an' groin shots over an' over.
> I nearly go.
> I nearly piss meself.
> 'Cos it's not normal fisticuffs any more, not Marquess of Queensberry.
> It's blood an' bone. (217)

The fight descends from a conventional bare-knuckle fighting contest based on technique and guile to a chaotic, animal frenzy. The 'blood an' bone' imagery recalls the disturbing picture of Anna's blood seeping over her amputated bones in *Anna's Ankle*. The reference to the Marquess of Queensberry rules invokes a respectable, gentlemanly code of conduct and may position middle-class spectators within this category, simultaneously elevating them above the ensuing encounter of savage aggression. The Howie Lee eventually defeats the Ladyboy and is himself thrown out of the window by Peaches, Ollie and Avalanche. The Rookie Lee observes his friend impaled on the railings: 'An' we stand an' we watch and he smiles an' I know why, it's 'cos he looks so ridiculous an' all's still an' quiet' (220).

The violence in the climactic episode is modified by O'Rowe's ironic humour. The Rookie Lee's comic flatulence, which in part precipitates the fight, and Dave McGee's vomiting and fainting, serve to parody the anticipated encounter. The impaling of the Howie Lee, which in another context may represent a tragic scene, is merely a stage for the Howie Lee to smile self-deprecatingly. Violence in *Howie the Rookie* is thus always deflected or displaced, and the perlocutionary effects on the audience are most likely to be a detached comic entertainment coupled with a pleasurable middle-class voyeurism of abject characters and their antics. Eamonn Jordan contends that

> the lenses of performance and irony introduce casualness, and a sort of defiant flippancy, when characters refuse to accept that they will be hurt by interaction. So it is almost a childish defiance, the two fingers to the trauma of existence, and a closing of the senses to darker realities (143).

O'Rowe's strategy of representing sex and violence is to disavow their bodily impact through linguistic displacement and comic irony. This may reflect the characters' own refusal to accept their abject circumstances, and their consequent embracing of fantasy and disengagement as means of spiritual survival.

Crestfall (2003) consists of three separate monologues delivered by Olive Day, Alison Ellis and Tilly McQuarrie, who reflect on a single day's events in a dystopian Irish town. Their separate narratives may be read as competing illocutionary acts, seeking to secure the perlocutionary effect of empathy from spectators.

Olive Day, while having sex with the Bru Ellis, reflects on the sexual abuse she suffered at the hands of her father and uncle: 'I grin to think of Daddy always broaching furtive but always failing, settling always for lap-sat stroking. Or Uncle Christopher succeeding, a little pain, a little bleeding. A little more determined than Daddy, he was the one to pop my cherry' (Plays: One 321). Olive's recollections appear to draw parallels between adult, consensual sex and incestuous sex. The absence of any attribution of blame to her father and uncle, whom she affectionately refers to as 'Daddy' and 'Uncle Christopher', betrays a tragic tone of ignorance of her own victimhood, and carries with it an illocutionary plea for empathy. The rhyming of 'succeeding' and 'bleeding', as well as the red imagery vivid in 'bleeding' and 'cherry', conveys the violence whilst insulating it in the assonant sounds of the spoken words.

When Olive crosses paths with Tilly McQuarrie, the perlocutionary effects on spectators of engendering empathy, arising from her disclosure of incest, are offset by her own genital violence towards Tilly: 'She has me by the hair. So I merely take a handful of crotch and squeeze, (Like so.)' (330). And when she returns home after meeting her lover Inchy Bassey, and finds that her husband Jungle has discovered that Poppin'eye is not his child, she submits to his physical assault in an attempt to facilitate his transformation into a vile being: 'This one time I'll play the prey and endure the pain, the destruction, in order to assist in your evolution' (335). Olive's oscillation between roles of victim and perpetrator of violence reflect her entrapment in a web of violence, instituted from an early age.

Alison Ellis' monologue bridges those of the two prostitutes and displays a greater awareness of the town's abject character. Her narrative is marked by a social and class consciousness, which carries the illocutionary force of persuading spectators to assign her a position above both Olive and Tilly. Alison describes finding her husband with another woman: 'They were on a bed, you see, and he was licking her out. (I know. That's a horrible phrase, but it's hard to watch your mouth, your Ps and Qs, after you've caught your husband right, in the middle of going down on some filthy cooze.)' (340). Alison's parenthetical address to the audience, which functions as a self-chastising aside and has the effect of foregrounding the foul language uttered by both Olive and Tilly, seeks favourable identification from middle-class spectators and attempts to relegate the prostitutes to abject social positions. Her projected middle-class attitudes have the effect of framing both the preceding monologue and final monologues from her position of social concern and propriety. When Alison opens the door to Benny Drumgoole, she and Olive Day see one another across the street. While Alison, in her monologue, constructs Olive as a 'slapper' and a 'horrible bitch' who mistreats her husband (342), Olive refers to Alison as a 'pious fucking cow' who is unaware that her husband has been having sex with her that day (327). Alison's moral propriety and Olive's sexual prowess and dominance may be read as competing addresses to the audience which have the effect of securing empathy for one (or neither or both) of the two characters. Alison's overt appeal to middle-class social codes, however, may not guarantee favourable uptake from middle-class spectators. It may carry a perlocutionary consequence of alienating those spectators from Alison and instead aligning themselves with Olive, motivated perhaps by a liberal understanding of socio-economic causes that have shaped the narratives of Olive and Tilly.

Tilly McQuarrie begins her narrative shortly after her violent encounter with Olive Day, the 'hateful agent' (354) of Tilly's tumble into a puddle. Tilly seeks to defend her aggression towards Olive by citing her problems of drug addiction: 'I was out of my mind with my need for the scourge, my thirst, so the deed was done in a surge of rage, of fucking despair' (354). The rhyming of 'scourge' and 'surge' in this passage links the affliction of drug addiction to her violent behaviour. Her drug addiction compels her to source drugs, or money to purchase drugs. And her search for money leads her to prostitute herself to 'johns' and to situations of violence. Trapped in a cycle of prostitution, drug addiction and violence, her monologue may be an attempt at self-determination and a breaking out of the cycle. The illocutionary appeal for empathy attempts to ameliorate Olive's construction of her as a 'cheeky junkie cunt' who occupies a position below Olive's place of 'position and prestige above the rank and file' (328).

Tilly positions herself as a helpless victim, in contrast to Olive's self-construction as 'a kind of queen of this fucking hole' (328), and Alison's as a moral guardian. The three competing illocutionary acts are likely to generate a range of perlocutionary effects, depending on the class and gender make-up of spectators. O'Rowe recalls and speculates on the several perlocutionary effects of the 2003 production of *Crestfall* at the Gate Theatre 'whose seats I can still hear banging up one by one as people fled the theatre in horror or outrage (or boredom? Or incomprehension?)' (*O'Rowe Plays: One* ix). Exiting the theatre terminates the theatrical contract between actors and spectators. The illocutionary acts of world-making, which seek to construct spectators as onlookers in that world, has therefore resulted in an 'infelicity' and 'misfired', to borrow Austin's terms. The 'misfire' occurred because the necessary conditions (i.e. the continued attendance and uptake of spectators) for the theatrical creation of a fictional world through speech have not been fulfilled. With fewer spectators, the possibilities for favourable uptake are diminished and the characters of *Crestfall* are ever more isolated.

Terminus (2007), in which three characters deliver, in sequence, three monologues each, is notable for its shift to a more explicit middle-class perspective and sensibility. In contrast to the worlds of *Howie the Rookie* and *Crestfall* where brutal acts largely comprise a necessary, unquestioned part of daily existence either to sustain or enhance one's violent reputation, acts of violence in *Terminus* are discretionary acts, either justified by moral crusade or undertaken for psychotic pleasure.

A's movement from a Samaritans call centre, emblematic of a social concern and awareness for public health issues, to a series of abject environments in search of her former student, may offer middle-class spectators an initial access point and subsequent narrative thread. A's impression of Helen's mother's house – 'suppose she's a drinker – the state of the place, the funk – or maybe a junkie' (*Terminus* 6) – reveals attitudes marking class superiority. And the verbal exchange with her mother underscores a class disparity between the two women:

> 'She's dead to me, love.'
> I ask why.

> 'For getting knocked up by some guy for one; for getting a taste for cunny, two.'
> 'For what?!'
> 'Honey, *you* know what they're like, those dykes, what they do. (*Terminus* 6-7)

A's questioning of the word 'cunny' is an effort to comprehend language not in her vocabulary, and a means of linguistically accessing a hitherto unfamiliar world. Her obtaining of information required to progress with her mission is thus intertwined with indoctrination into an unfamiliar, abject language.

After being beaten unconscious in 'a sinister-looking pub' (22) by Celine and her accomplices, A determines to 'chasten Celine, to break her down, to punish and purge her for what she's done' (35). Her humiliation of a perverted bartender in order to ascertain Helen's whereabouts and her descent through the door in the floor of the pub suggests a reversal of roles from victim to perpetrator of violence: 'Instead, my hands whip out and grip her face like a vice and my thumbs find their way to her eyes and I dig them in and they begin to collapse into her skull as she tries to pull away and pleads for me to stop, to no avail' (35). A's initial construction as a socially concerned former teacher is dismantled through an act of barbaric, vigilante violence. Middle-class spectators, originally positioned to identify with A, may be alienated as A's blinding and fatal bludgeoning of Celine outdoes the brutality of the earlier narrated violence.

If A's journey takes her through inner city and suburban Dublin, B embarks on a fantastic adventure with a winged creature composed of worms, the earthly form of a soul who was sold to the devil in return for the soul-giver's receiving a prodigious singing talent. When she falls from the arm of a crane at a construction site, she is rescued by the creature, who claims to be the soul of C. Their ensuing relationship, based on mutual respect and shared warmth, throws into relief the abusive relationship between Helen and Celine, which is characteristic of social relations in other represented abject settings: 'he takes my hand and gives me a look so understanding that it doesn't seem ugly in any way to let him hug me' (27). Their post-coital conversation also indicates a respect for sex that elevates it above the perfunctory, casual sex of C and other O'Rowe characters:

> 'I think I'm in love with you.'
> 'Well,' I say, 'that's typical of a guy; to fall for the very first girl you fuck.'
> 'Have sex with,' he corrects with, suddenly coy.
> 'Make love to,' I say, enjoying our ease with each other (40)

The quick retreat from the use of the word 'fuck' as a description of their encounter, and the progression from 'have sex with' to finally, 'make love to' illustrates a distancing from casual or even violent or perverted sexual encounters experienced by A, when Joe White the bartender uses her naked body as a visual aid for his masturbation, or C, who disembowels a girl whilst having sex with her.

C is represented as an articulate, astute young man whose calculated, psychotic behaviour is emphasized when he says 'And the next few hours just fucking rock' (15) to describe his love-making with a girl he meets at a disco, followed by the admission later in his narrative that he 'speared her from the rear and, while being fucked, she bucked and brayed, I took my blade and stuck it in, then used my hand to grope about and pull her nethers inside out' (17). The seduction of the girl and the concealment from her of his murderous intent seem to correspond with his narrative manipulation of spectators, who belatedly understand that 'what fucking rocks' is not the love-making but the killing.

C, whose attitude to violence recalls the sadistic narrator in *Anna's Ankle*, positions himself as superior by referring to the three men in the car park as 'losers', before killing two of them and pursuing the third. His psychotic behaviour is reflected by the performance of the narrative: 'Number one, I split from crown to chin. He screams and, relishing the din, I hew numbers two across the throat and gloat as he gouts arterial spray and flays and, Jaysus, pirouettes as jets of blood arc round him, like some kind of fountain' (15). C's movement in a car from Cashel to Dublin, with various violent episodes, bears all the hallmarks of Hollywood serial killer road movies, in which progression through towns and countryside may be read as the protagonist's deteriorating mental state. His craving for fame and recognition, which remains unrequited following his Faustian pact, seeks fulfilment in a series of violent episodes likely to attract extensive media attention. After he parks his truck in the loading bay at the Jervis Centre, he slips by 'the delivery guys, with ease, distracted as they are by some chick without clothes in the *Daily Star*, I suppose, the *Sun*, one of those' (46). The motivation for seeking recognition is founded upon a self-construction as gifted, unique and superior, and a construction of all others as subordinates, a superiority which finds expression through the reiteration of class distinctions. C's long-awaited opportunity to sing publicly is paradoxically occasioned by his fatal reunion with the soul that he sold for that gift.

The monologues of *Terminus* constitute spectators as passengers alongside the three protagonists as they journey to their destinations by foot, car, truck, train and air. The sense of movement and travelling may be said to bring spectators from an origin point of safety (a Samaritans call centre, an apartment, a community centre) to a destination of unsettling proximity to, and participation in, acts of gratuitous violence. O'Rowe's monologues in *Terminus* disrupt spectatorial complacency through constant movement and restlessness, along with gratuitous acts of sex and violence. In this way, he removes voyeuristic lenses that were present in *Howie the Rookie* and *Crestfall* and challenges middle-class spectators to identify with acts of barbarity.

I will now turn to the theories of Judith Butler to conclude the chapter with an analysis of *Howie the Rookie* and *Crestfall* and their largely abject contexts. Butler's theories of performativity differ significantly from Austin in that she does not posit a stable, self-determining, centred subject who wilfully chooses to perform speech acts. Instead, she theorizes that when subjects perform speech acts or gestures, they inevitably cite regulatory laws, which carry the force of regulating the subjects who cite them, including their gender and race. The subject that does the citing is not in control of the cited laws because the laws carry their own histories: 'a reiteration of norms which precede, constrain and exceed the performer' (176). In the act of citing, however, there is an opportunity to resignify the cited laws. Butler further claims that the 'exclusionary matrix by which subjects are formed thus requires the simultaneous production of a domain of abject beings, those who are not yet 'subjects,' but who form the constitutive outside to the domain of the subject' (xiii). In other words, a domain of 'abject beings' is necessary to constitute and support a domain of 'subjects'.

Following Butler's terminology, the depicted worlds in *Howie the Rookie* and *Crestfall* may be said to contain 'abject beings'. If Butler is referring primarily to gender in her argument, we may read O'Rowe's abject beings as being deprived of full subject status due to the construction of their class. And when one again considers the composition of audiences who view these plays, mostly educated and middle-class, we may interpret two separate domains interacting as part of a theatrical relationship between actor and spectator: the abject domains of O'Rowe's underworlds and the privileged domain of middle-class, educated, economically protected spectators. If according to Butler, the privileged domain depends on the abject domain to constitute itself, we may suggest that middle-class identities are in some way kept intact by the abject beings they are viewing.

The Howie Lee appears to be trapped in an abject world of casual violence, drinking and juvenile horse-play around the community. Although his father is employed, there is neither reference to his own job nor any attempt to find employment. His father wants to go to his local pub, The Fort, 'because he's nothin' better to do. Nothin' better, 'cos he *knows* no better' (182). There is no evidence, however, that the Howie has any ambitions greater than his father. And his friends exhibit no signs of aspiring to anything other than retributive physical assaults, womanizing, drinking, smoking and watching videos. The boredom and anomie portrayed in *Howie the Rookie* appears to generate an appetite amongst its characters for any thrill that can keep it at bay. However, the death of Mousey Lee, and the Howie's culpability for his death, appear to remove any hope for a resignification of the abjection that the Howie and the other characters experience. The Howie says to himself to 'Keep movin'. Get away. Get away from that house, that street' (201) but we discover that the Howie is not metaphorically moving away from a life of idleness, but merely walking away and embroiling himself in a feud between the Rookie Lee and Ladyboy.

The Rookie Lee's narrative ends with the death of the Howie Lee, his 'namesake the name of Lee, me saviour' (221), followed by the viewing on a video of the lifeless Mousey Lee, whose image closes the play. Images of death are dominant and by ending his narrative on the Howie Lee's couch, there is a suggestion that he may be destined to play out an unenlightened cycle of violence himself, as Howie's murder by Ollie, Peaches and Avalanche remains to be avenged.

Olive Day in *Crestfall* confesses that the sexual abuse she suffered as a child is a cause of her current reckless sexual behaviour: 'And in the years that followed I became a righteous sexual fiend, and wallowed in my many filthy rendezvous' (321). Her assertion of dominance over Tilly, to reaffirm her position within a hierarchy of prostitutes managed by her lover Inchy Bassey, may be read as a citation of violent means of control that was exercised upon her as a child. Her submission to Jungle's beating and her wish that her husband will 'be vile and, in being so, to belong, to fit' (335) signals an inability to envision any existence without violence as its currency. 'Fitting in' to the world of *Crestfall* invariably means conforming to brutal behavioural norms.

If Olive Day buckles under violent normative pressures and is thus consigned to interminable cycles of violence, Alison Ellis fails to adequately engage the realities around her and instead retreats into a cocoon of self-delusion. She is aware on some level of her husband's infidelity with Olive while she hugs Philip, when she says that 'something now gnaws at me like a rat, something I've forgotten, though, caught up in this misbegotten embrace, I'm happy to let it go for now' (353). The Bru Ellis has, it seems, renounced his philandering lifestyle and attempted to protect his son from the Deegan brothers, but Alison remains unaware of her husband's transformation. Trying to recover her son from his emotional withdrawal, she persists with her faith in prayer. But as the desecrated, handless statue on Marais Hill symbolizes, belief in the efficacy of prayer and in a divine will is misplaced and only bound to prolong her and her family's endurance of the world of *Crestfall*.

Tilly McQuarrie, firmly in the grip of drug addiction, is perhaps the character of the trio for whom there is least hope of escape. She is desperate for 'that ever-elusive strain that'll bless me with bliss, ease my pain for a time at least' (355) but without clients, she cannot obtain money to pay for drugs. When she succeeds in meeting with a client, she is violently assaulted and threatened with further violence by her pimp, Inchy Bassey. After causing the demise of Olive Day, Inchy Bassey and the Deegan brothers, Tilly finds a moment of happiness with Poppin'eye: 'And the kids upriver jump back in, and the sun shines on, and the splashing and squealing recommences, and I frown at the child, 'cos common sense is saying he'll soon be taken away from me. And, of course, it's true. But, live for the moment. Live for the now' (369).

Tilly's playing with Poppin'eye in the river may not change the abject conditions of her life but it offers a glimpse of those possibilities. The abject contexts may not challenge cultural privilege but it cannot be said to entirely fetishize violence either. The interface between abject and privileged domains may produce moments of pleasurable voyeurism for middle-class spectators as they look down upon abject worlds, but these are offset by simple moments of tenderness, connection and warmth, which have the potential to remove class barriers between the domains, if only momentarily.

Austin's and Butler's theories of performativity, despite significant differences, both assert the power of language to produce a state of affairs, rather than simply describe them. Language in O'Rowe's monologue plays has been shown to determine the level of engagement with the worlds of the plays by middle-class audiences. The film-making terminology of *Anna's Ankle* facilitates a nauseating participation in the making of a snuff video. *Terminus'* monologues transport spectators from protected environments to sites of violence. The language and abject environments depicted in *Howie the Rookie* and *Crestfall* resist access to middle-class spectators and instead possibly position them as voyeurs overlooking the action. Austin's speech-act theory limits itself to language and in this regard, O'Rowe has skilfully constructed different worlds with his monologues. Butler's concern with the ethical and political dimension of language and its constituting powers highlights in O'Rowe's work the constructed and performative nature of class (as opposed to it being a subject's fixed and essential attribute). Butler's theories may therefore offer ways in which class, identifiable through language or otherwise, may be viewed as mere constructions and hence break down barriers between spectators and the characters they are viewing.

Works Cited

Austin, J.L. *How to Do Things with Words*. Second ed. Oxford: Oxford University Press, 1976.

Bennett, Susan. *Theatre Audiences: A Theory of Production and Reception*. London: Routledge, 1990.

Jordan, Eamonn. 'Look Who's Talking, Too: The Duplicitous Myth of Naive Narrative.' *Monologues: Theatre, Performance, Subjectivity*. Ed. Wallace, Clare. Prague: Litteraria Pragensia, 2006. 330.

Lonergan, Patrick. *Theatre and Globalization: Irish Drama in the Celtic Tiger Era*. Basingstoke: Palgrave Macmillan, 2009.

O'Rowe, Mark. *Plays: One*. London: Nick Hern Books, 2011.

---. *Terminus*. London: Nick Hern Books, 2007.

---. *Anna's Ankle*: 'Unpublished Script.' Dublin, 1997.

Singleton, Brian. *Masculinities and the Contemporary Irish Theatre*. Basingstoke: Palgrave Macmillan, 2011.

7 | From 'Up-Yer-Hole' Theatre to the Shakesqueer: *Made in China* (2001) and *Henry IV Part I* (2002).

Emma Creedon

As this collection goes to press, Druid Theatre has just opened a new version of the four plays of Shakespeare's *Henriad* by Mark O'Rowe, in collaboration with the Lincoln Center Festival, New York, in 2015. The seeds of this ambitious project can be traced to O'Rowe's staging of a version of *Henry IV* for the Abbey Theatre's Peacock stage in 2002. This was a rare dramatization of one of Shakespeare's history plays in Dublin, and critics responded favourably, particularly praising the production's cinematic vigour; 'a snappy, stylish production, more Guy Ritchie than William Shakespeare' (7) wrote Roberta Gray for the *Sunday Tribune*, '[O'Rowe] brings to the stage a Tarantino-like energy' (5), Ciaran Carty claimed in the same paper. Fintan O'Toole likewise praised the production's 'cinematic rhythm' (*The Irish Times*).

Made in China (2001), which was produced at the Peacock Theatre the year before, pre-empted the Irish playwright's thematic interests in *Henry IV Part I*. In an interview with Prof. Patrick Lonergan at the Synge Summer School in 2013, O'Rowe attributed the filmic quality of his play to the director Gerard Stembridge's experience of working as both a screenwriter and film director. However, the heightened physicality and hyperbolic violence of *Made in China* is also evident in the celluloid, graphic quality of *Henry IV*. This chapter argues that *Made in China* revisits a number of the key themes as posited in *Henry IV Part I*, notably the legitimacy of rulership, the shackles of inheritance and the cogency of loyalty. My intention here is to highlight how a consideration of Shakespeare's text can help to re-define and contextualize O'Rowe's concerns in his earlier play.

Made in China is set in a surreal gangland metropolis, a twentieth century re-imagining of the Falstaffian tavern underworld, suggested to be Dublin by the distinct local dialect, but without any definite local markers. Hughie is a member of an Echelon gang, answerable to the local Hooligan chief, Puppacat whose impending arrival contributes to the escalating suspense in the play. In the first act, Hughie's mother is fighting for her life in intensive care after a car accident. Sent to beat up Bernie Denk on a 'job', Hughie discovers a 'gift' from Puppacat: the driver of the car that hit his mother, '[t]ied up in the chair, minus *teeth*' (39). According to Kilby, Puppacat's mule, his boss

> [d]ragged the fuck up to Bernie's, set up the Puppa-surprise. Surprise took time an' thought, took plannin' out of goodness, the benevolent Puppacat, magnanimous cunt *like* him, helpin' out his *man*. Givin' him justice an' payback an' the chance of some righteous batterin'. (41)

However, when Hughie refuses Puppacat's 'favour', Kilby takes umbrage and threatens to initiate Paddy into the Echelon tribe in his place. The second act takes place a week later, following Hughie's mother's (Dolly's) funeral. The loutish Kilby is priming Paddy as a protégé, a task he approaches with the (literal) zealous dedication of a Sensei to his pupil. The simmering violence of the play erupts when it emerges that Hughie had previously played an active role in an attack on Kilby; he was anally penetrated with a pool cue, which left him in a coma for three days. However, it is Hughie's insinuation that Kilby's cherished blonde perm is a direct legacy from the attack that catalyses the chaos:

> KILBY: That's a real fuckin' paid for perm, man, groomed an' styled an' you're a liar. You're an insidious little fuck, have to conquer with lies an' shitstirrin'. The badge is down now, you hear me? (*Mimes throwing down the badge.*) The tin star is well an' truly on the floor an' Kilby's fuckin' ragin'!! Ragin' like a beast an' ready to fuckin' maim!!! (78)

The title of *Made in China* suggests, from the onset, an interest in the phoney, the spurious, the kitsch, even. In the aforementioned interview with Patrick Lonergan, O'Rowe stated that the 'cartoonish' nature of the premiere production of *Made in China* was a deliberate attempt to recreate the world hinted at in *Howie the Rookie*. Yet the playwright was adamant in his emphasis that the works of Samuel Beckett, Harold Pinter, and Tennessee Williams have always been major influences on his work whilst the cartoons of 'Bugs Bunny' have not. Likewise, O'Rowe stated that although Kung-Fu movies may have inspired *Made in China*, he was also extremely well read in classic literature, as evident in his interest in Shakespeare.

Henry IV Part I is a play less concerned with its namesake than the escapades of Prince Hal and the character of Puppacat operates in a similar manner in O'Rowe's play. In a review of his version of *Henry IV* at the Peacock Theatre, Fintan O'Toole wrote that '[t]he King here is not so much a character as a formal expression of power.' In a similar manner, Fintan Walsh argues that Puppacat is 'less a dramatic character than a symbolic device or master signifier in the generation and stability of meaning in the play world.' (61) However, Puppacat could also be interpreted as the Falstaffian figure of *Made in China*, the 'villainous abominable misleader of youth' (*1 Henry IV* 2.4.457), and the symbolic father for whose approval and attention the other characters compete. In this comparison, Hughie figures as the Prince Hal figure, Paddy as Poins and Kilby as Hotspur. Whereas Falstaff's gross and excessive physicality is made implicit in Shakespeare's play by Prince Hal's numerous references to his 'fatness', the authoritative figure of Puppacat in *Made in China*, like the elusive Godot, never materializes on the stage at all. Gerard Stembridge's programme note for O'Rowe's interpretation of Shakespeare's play emphasized Falstaff's centrality to the play's action: '[...] it is around the characters of Falstaff and Hotspur that Shakespeare constructs the real dramatic meat of *Henry IV (Part One)* in the form of two memorable triangles; the father with two potential sons, and the son with two potential fathers.'

In her study on *Shakespeare and Twentieth-Century Irish Drama*, Rebecca Steinberger cites Mashey Bernstein's definition of Sean O'Casey's Dublin as 'a world poised constantly on the brink of disaster and yet sustained by a comic impulse, the ability to take serious matters and see the humor in them' (45). Steinberger thus describes Shakespeare as the 'progenitor for this motif in drama starting with *I Henry IV*' (45), drawing comparisons between the tragi-comedy of Shakespeare's play and the similar oscillation between humour and disaster that the setting of Dublin seems to elicit in drama. Bernstein argues that a Dublin location facilitates, or even invites, an irreverent attitude towards misfortune. Taken to the extreme in *Made in China*, the audience is encouraged to laugh at atrociously violent acts. Descriptions such as Hughie's account of Kilby's anal impalement are both disturbing and darkly funny: 'Welters of gore, there was, fuckin' *geysers* of blood spurtin', *sprayin*' out of both ends of him, hole *an*' mouth. That right, Kilby? Gurglin' like a blocked drain' (73). Yet such accounts are so removed from reality that they are relegated to the realm of the grotesque and thus to fantasy. The proliferation of 'high' vocabulary, interspersed with 'low' urban slang, lyricism juxtaposed with profanity, mirrors the seemingly irreverent approach to violence in the play.

This linguistic incongruity recalls *I Henry IV*, which, as Fintan O'Toole has noted

> is an experimental piece in which Shakespeare uses prose dialogue—the medium of the common man—far more than ever before. Even the poetry, especially that of the self-consciously plain speaking Hotspur, is lean, direct, deliberately anti-poetical. When we get the formal rhetoric of the court it is usually in the form of parody, as Falstaff and Prince Hal engage in a continual burlesque of proper princely speech.

Henry's opening lines are particularly violent; he speaks of civil war and how peace will now reign yet the imagery of 'intestine shock' and 'civil butchery' (ll 12-13), recalling similar images of corporeal mutilation in *Made in China*. O'Toole's identification of a 'burlesque of proper princely speech' has equal relevance; the stylized language in *Made in China* is similarly a 'lean, direct, deliberately anti-poetical' (O'Toole) type of poetry which combines the musical cadences of 'Dublinese' expressions such as 'pissed-off-ness', 'chunkhead' and 'slaggin'' with curiously antiquated terms such as 'beset', 'echelon', 'wrath', and 'behoof'. The language of *Made in China* is particularly theatrical and self-consciously performative.

O'Rowe's version of *I Henry IV* revisited similar themes of violence and performative masculinity as investigated in *Made in China*.[9] According to Valerie Traub

> [I]n the histories and tragedies masculine identity is deadly serious. The fate of the nations depends on male strength, valour, and rational judgement. The development of the young man into a leader other man will follow is the theme of *1* and *2 Henry IV*, as the 'madcap Prince of Wales' learns to forgo adolescent pastimes, gain the stature and authority to succeed his father, and to bring to rest civil strife. Prince Hal's development requires that he hone his rhetorical expertise, prove himself in battle against a rival 'brother,' Hotspur, and banish pleasure as embodied by the 'jolly knight,' Falstaff. His attainment of all three depends on his ability to manipulate other men's ideas of manhood as becomes clear in his effort to rouse his weary troops to battle with the promise of a cross-class brotherhood. (137)

---

[9] As evidenced from videos of the performance from The Abbey Theatre archives and from critical responses to the production

Made in China places similar weight on 'male strength, valour, and rational judgment', the demonstration of physical supremacy, and the 'manipulation of other men's ideas of manhood' that Traub identifies above. As a development of this, Karen Fricker has drawn parallels between the theatricality of the language and the performance of masculinity in *Made in China*. Fricker interprets language as a weapon and notes that '[s]peaking functions as a form of sparring' (91) in a similar manner to the performative verbal battles for supremacy in *Henry IV*. Indeed, *Made in China* interrogates the indeterminacy of gender identities and sexualities, as Fricker and Fintan Walsh have investigated. The male characters in *Made in China* are represented as hypermasculine yet a distinct homoeroticism is evident in the text, as evinced by Kilby and Paddy's illicit 'sucking' of Hughie's 'salty' knix-knax and the fact that Paddy's penis habitually escapes from his underwear in the first act. However, this is complicated by the fact that the male body elicits disgust; Kilby refers to Paddy's penis as a 'dirty wiggly thing' (37) yet he is obsessed with anal penetration, (so much so that Walsh has deemed O'Rowe's drama 'Up-yer-hole theatre' (59)). On the other hand, Kilby speaks of his desire to give Copper Dolan a '[g]ood buggerin'', '[n]ot in a sexual way' but with a '[p]owerful motion he wouldn't like' (33), whilst the climactic action of the play revolves around Kilby's attempts to bugger Hughie with an umbrella. Thus, anal penetration is not a homoerotic act in this play but an act of torture, never consensual and always forced. Kilby's obsession with the act, nonetheless, and his re-appropriation of it from the sexual to the caustic, is evidence of his attempts to consume the dissident 'Other'; as Walsh writes of this play '[w]hen normative masculinity is threatened, the disruptive element must be rejected or incorporated for order to be restored' (58).[10]

In *Made in China*, the very challenge to the presentation of a hegemonic authoritative singular masculinity rejects the binary between the homo and hetero-sexual and could be interpreted as more

---

[10] Furthermore, in light of the filmic quality of both pieces, as emphasized by the critical responses, Gus Van Sant's cinematic translation of the *Henriad*, *My Own Private Idaho* (1991), offers an interesting comparison, particularly regarding the film's treatment of the indeterminacy of gender identities and sexuality, the quest for authenticity, and finally, the opportunity for reformation. According to Kenneth Rothwell, *My Own Private Idaho* is an example of new 'Shakesqueer' trends in Shakespearean criticism (192). The film is an interesting exploration of new familial reconfigurations and political and sexual transgressions in a pastiche, and at times self-reflexive, postmodern form.

in line with the fluid sexualities of the Renaissance era. It is not my intention to contribute to this already rich debate on the representation of masculinity in O'Rowe's work as discussed by Fricker and Walsh, and others in this volume, but rather to signal to the performative nature of gender as indicative of pretence and a lack of authenticity.Furthermore, the world created in *Made in China* also borrows from Shakespeare the carnivalesque, the anti-authoritarian and the politically subversive, particularly in the representation of women in the play. The men admonish the character of Nancy, for instance, for her indiscretions with Bernie Denk at Dolly's funeral. She pays for 'bein' a slut' (54) by having her prosthetic leg stolen by Hughie while Bernie is not reprimanded for *his* role in the act. The ferociousness of female sexuality and desire is particularly Shakespearean as Nancy is portrayed as a grotesque whore, powerless against her forceful libido and, bearing only one leg, her body becomes a grotesque phallic symbol. According to Fricker, 'women function in *Made in China* as maternal icons or grotesque, oversexualized objects of disgust and ridicule' (87). Furthermore, in the carnivalesque, the body becomes a site of transgressive representation and revolt: 'The grotesque body is the open, protruding, extended, secreting body, the body of becoming, process and change' (Russo 325). Similarly, Traub observes that in Shakespearean drama:

> The body is also a site of disease, and Shakespeare frequently employs venereal disease to figure what is wrong with social and erotic relations. Images of syphilis (called 'the French pox', in a nationalistic displacement of responsibility) crop up whenever prostitution is invoked.' (140)

This is reflected in the description of Hughie's 'scaldy stomach of stress' (7), the physical manifestation of anxiety as a metonym for society's ills, of something rotten in the state of Dublin. Moreover, the language of *I Henry IV* also contains images of corporeal decay and fragmentation:

> ...Those opposèd eyes,
> Which, like the meteors of a troubled heaven,
> All of one nature, of one substance bred,
> Did lately meet in the intestine shock
> And furious close of civil butchery (ll 12-13)

O'Rowe also exploits the sexual charge of boy gangs; in this gangland culture, the names of the characters are branded – Puppacat,

CopperDolan, even Kilby refers to himself in the third person – he believes his own facade and mythologization.

The performance of masculinity in this play dictates that pain is something to endure, a durability that Kilby describes as 'echelon incarnate' (82) as the account of his buggering with a pool cue testifies. 'I attained a knowin' state that day, I did, day I was impaled. Somethin' youse cunts'll never understand. Mastery was attained; understandin', balance ... State a monk of Shaolin reaches when he lifts that giant urn .... Bear the marks, I do .... They're *my* dragon an' tiger, see, 'cos I *am* Shaolin' (82). Kilby's identity has been consumed by his own self-classification as a martial arts fighter. He directs Paddy not to smile at Puppacat, to demonstrate how 'vicious' he is (52). The concept of 'Brotherhood' is likewise deemed a performance by the climatic 'outing' of CopperDolan's jacket as fake. The fallacious nature of the jacket, the fact that, as we discover, the 'Brotherhood of the Guards' translates as 'Made in China', is a concrete metaphor for the superficiality of the idea of Brotherhood as a romanticized aspiration of masculinity. The title of this play is hence a metonym for the counterfeit, introducing themes of deception and the positing of authenticity. By 'labelling' the play 'Made in China', the title is a self-reflective comment on the superficiality of the performance itself; it is a pre-mediated construct and is packaged, whole and ready to be duplicated. Paddy likewise signals to a 'real' Kilby, beyond the performance: 'Kilby's sensitive man, [...]. All the fucker needs is patience, bit of understandin', whatever you get *behind* the exterior, the mask, get the *real* Kilby' (59). However, Paddy has bought into the Echelon's 'style,'—'[...] I'll tell you what style is. *Guru* style. It's a durable dragon fist [...] Kilby's jacket that Dolan stroked' (63). Just as Hughie has invested in John Rocha designer shirts, Hughie's revelation to Paddy about the jacket's inauthenticity shatters the latter's romanticized view of the Echelon posse.

As an extension of the counterfeit nature of 'brotherhood', there are suggestions in *Made in China* that Paddy and Hughie share a mother and are thus *actual* brothers. Paddy's preference for wearing a snorkel and Hughie's admonishment that he can't dress himself properly (45) imply that Paddy is either a much younger man or that he is mentally weak. Thus, as well as satisfying the Hal/Poins/Falstaff pairing, Hughie and Kilby could also be read as potential father figures to Paddy, a dynamic that seems to echo the Hal/ Henry/ Falstaff paternal drama in *I Henry IV*. Paddy initially rejects the insinuation that Hughie is his brother in Act Two, yet seems to miraculously remember in the final stages of the play as he lies helpless on the floor with two broken legs:

> Yes, it just came to me. We were in the sittin' room ... Ah, shit! We'd, we'd hot whiskeys an' dry roasters, am I right?, Peanuts, an' I started ... I spilt my whiskey, started, cryin' 'cos of the stress of the day, man, the events that were in it ... started cryin' an' she hugged me, I remember, man an' said it was okay. It was okay because she's be ... (*In pain.*) Agh!
> ...
> Said she'd be me mother ... long as you were my brother. (86)

However, Hughie corrects him: 'Long as you were mine, Paddy. Long as you were mine, an' as of today, man ... you're Kilby's, aren't you. Tell *him* your problems' (86). Hughie's words suggest both the paternal rejection of a son, and sibling rivalry. For, as Wiseman writes of the *Henriad*, '... men rely on one another to support structures of male dominance, [but] they must also be willing to kill one another' for '[i]n the internecine bloodshed of the histories, rival 'brothers' vie for the crown' (138).

Wiseman's words suggest a blurring of the lines between the Oedipal struggle for kinship and male sibling rivalry. In *Made in China*, Dolly's death signals a new appropriation of the concept of the 'family', pertaining to what Fredrick Jameson has described as a 'degraded Utopian content of the family paradigm', which 'ultimately unmasks itself as the survival of more archaic forms of repression and sexism and violence' (34). At the play's conclusion, Hughie must reject his 'brother' Paddy as well as the Echelon franchise that Paddy aspires to be part of, much in the same manner that Prince Hal discards Poins and the underworld of delinquency with which he associates in *Henry IV Part I*. However, Falstaff's 'staging' of his fake death at the end of *Henry IV Part I* is also relevant here. Falstaff exclaims:

> To die is to be a counterfeit, for he is but the counterfeit of a man who hath not the life of a man; but to counterfeit dying, when a man thereby liveth, is to be no counterfeit, but the true and perfect image of life indeed. The better part of valor is discretion, in the which better part I have sav'd my life. (V. iv 121-124)

According to Ellen M. Caldwell, Shakespeare's play

> challenges princely power as representational, iconic, and false. Sir John Falstaff espouses a 'reformationist' distrust of the image and reflects, in his powerful combination of corporeal presence and punishing rhetoric, a proto-Protestant scorn for ornamentation and hypocrisy' (218-219).

The notion of the counterfeit is a pervasive theme in *Henry IV Part I* and *Made in China* In Shakespeare's play, this is initiated by Prince Hal's self-conscious speech in Act One, Scene Two in which he announces that he will exaggerate his wayward behaviour so that his subsequent reformation into a princely leader will be all the more admirable:

> And like bright metal on a sullen ground,
> My reformation, glittering o'er my fault,
> Shall show more goodly, and attract more eyes
> Than that which hath no foil to set it off.
> I'll so offend, to make offence a skill,
> Redeeming time when men think least I will. (1.2 210-215)

Prince Hal's words denote a conscious contrivance of identity in the manipulation of his public persona, mirroring Hughie's identity as an Echelon member. Furthermore the notion of costuming in *Made in China* also suggests the contrivance of identity. Walsh notes of O'Rowe's play,

> [a]s the coat does not read 'Brotherhood of the Guard', the sovereignty of Kilby and Copper Dolan's masculinity is simultaneously brought into question through an inferred masquerade. Hughie explicitly draws attention to the unravelling of normative identity by saying that the disclosure of the insignia's meaning had the effect of 'queerin' things up' (64).

Walsh also observes how characters habitually shed clothes in this play and labels it a 'drama of undressing' (62). Hughie's initial behaviour toward Paddy is affectionate, helping him to remove his snorkel jacket (3). As posited by Shakespeare's *Hamlet* 'the clothes maketh the man' and the performative nature of male identity in *Made in China* is given dramatic realization in Paddy practicing his 'audition' for Puppacat. However, the dramatic action of both *Made in China* and *Henry IV* revolves around misplaced loyalty. Henry has failed to repay the favour of Percy's helping him to overthrow his predecessors just as Hughie declines to acknowledge Puppacat's 'gift' to him. Both plays feature the reformation of the central character as prompted by the rejection of a domineering patriarch. In *Made in China*, it is Hughie's rejection of a violent masculinity that catalyses his liberation from the Echelon league when he refuses to carry out a 'batterin'' on the driver of the car responsible for his mother's hospitalization and subsequent death. This rejection offers the possibility of liberation from and transcendence over the shackles of outmoded essentialist gender norms. At the end of *Made in China*, Hughie is the only man left standing, recalling the final scenes of *I Henry IV* during which Hal stands over the bodies of his dead rival Hotspur and Falstaff, lying '*as if he were dead*' (V.4 75). There is also the suggestion of redemption, and the termination of cyclical systems of aggressive masculinity, in Paddy's refusal of violence at the end of the play. The play's final stage directions document his inability to prove himself in battle. Whereas violence is suggested to be innate to Kilby – 'to strike back's me nature' (50), Paddy is not 'vicious' (52) enough to be initiated into the Echelon tribe:

> PADDY crawls over to KILBY, very slowly, shouting in pain as he goes, sits beside him, picks up the baseball bat. He starts crying, stops abruptly, composes himself, looks at KILBY. Long pause. He raises the bat. Hold. Brings it down on his lap, begins weeping again as the lights fade down to darkness. (87)

The ending of *Made in China* sees Paddy lying incapacitated and vulnerable to Puppacat's inevitable wrath (the noise of Puppacat's encroachment was explicitly exaggerated in the Peacock production in 2002). Hughie's desertion of Paddy mirrors Prince Hal's rejection of Falstaff on the verge of being crowned as Henry V: 'I know thee not, old man. Fall to thy prayers' (5.5.47).

On Druid's forthcoming collaboration with O'Rowe on Shakespeare's *Henriad*, Garry Hynes has commented on Druid's website: 'This is a great story of families and wars and the making of nations ... the question we are asking is how, in the context of the historical relationship between Ireland and England, do we as Irish artists produce these plays today?' O'Rowe's staging of *I Henry IV* in 2002 may have prematurely answered Hynes' question. Although not an explicit commentary on Ireland's relationship with England, the foregrounding of the similarities of *I Henry IV*, a Shakespearean history play on the successive reigns of imperial monarchs, to *Made in China*, a play set distinctly in a surreally rendered Dublin, reveals the universality of Shakespeare's themes. Furthermore, the conclusion of Stembridge's programme note for O'Rowe's version of *I Henry IV* suggests the play's relevance to an Irish audience: 'So, *Henry IV (Part One)*; it's all about Fathers and Sons then? Now that's something an Irish play-going audience can appreciate.'

Works Cited

Caldwell, Ellen M. ' 'Banish All the Wor(l)d': Falstaff's Iconoclastic Threat to Kinship in *1 Henry IV*.' *Renaissance* 59: 4 (2007): 218-219.

Carty, Ciaran. 'From Stage to Screen', *The Sunday Tribune* 1 December 2002: 5.

Fricker, Karen. 'Same Old Show: The Performance of Masculinity in Conor McPherson's *Port Authority* and Mark O'Rowe's *Made in China*', *The Irish Review* 29 (2002): 84-94.

Gray, Roberta. 'Shakespeare Over Lock, Stock and Two Smoking Barrels.' Rev. of *I Henry IV*, dir. Jimmy Fay. *The Sunday Tribune* 1 December 2002: 7.

Jameson, Fredrick. *Signatures of the Visible*. New York and London: Routledge, 1992.

O'Rowe, Mark. *Made in China*. London: Nick Hern, 2001.

O'Toole, Fintan. Rev. of *I Henry IV*, dir. Jimmy Fay. *The Irish Times* 28 November 2002.

Rothwell, Kenneth S. *A History of Shakespeare on Screen: A Century of Film and Television*. Cambridge: Cambridge UP, 2004.

Russo, Mary. 'Female Grotesques: Carnival and Theory.' *Writing on the Body: Female Embodiment and Feminist Theory*. ed. Katie Conboy et al. New York: Routledge, 1994. 318-336.

Shakespeare, William. *Henry IV (Part One)*, ed. P.H. Davison. London: Penguin Book,1996.

Steinberger, Rebecca. *Shakespeare and Twentieth Century Irish Drama: Conceptualizing Identity and Staging Boundaries*. Hampshire: Ashgate, 2008.

Stembridge, Gerard. Programme Note for *Henry IV (Part One)*. The Abbey Theatre, 2002.

Traub, Valerie. 'Gender and Sexuality in Shakespeare.' *The Cambridge Companion to Shakespeare*. Ed. Margreta de Grazia and Stanley Wells. Cambridge: Cambridge UP, 2001: 129-146.

Walsh, Fintan. *Masculinity and the Performance of Crisis*. London: Palgrave Macmillan, 2010.

Wiseman, Susan. 'The Family Tree Motel: Subliming Shakespeare in *My Own Private Idaho*.' *Shakespeare, the Movie: Popularizing the Plays on Film, TV, and Video*. Ed. Lynda E. Boose and Richard Burt. London: Routledge, 1997.

8 | At the Terminus in the Brain: Illusions of consciousness in Mark O'Rowe's *Terminus*

Marie Kelly

In the middle of Mark O'Rowe's *Terminus* (2007) a young woman identified as B describes being snatched from the jaws of death by a demon who tells her that:

> I'm a soul, but the body I lived in is'nt dead. I was sold to Satan for the going rate and I'm here to reclaim my erstwhile 'host', I suppose he's called.[11]

Alongside many of his peers in Irish theatre Mark O'Rowe's writing has wrestled with the notion of soul, spirit, and mind. At the centre of this is the implication of the Cartesian *cogito* which splits consciousness away from the body and assumes an 'inner man' with the potential of existing beyond the moment of death. According to Réne Descartes

> From that I knew that I was a substance, the whole essence or nature of which is to think, and that for its existence there is no need of any place, nor does it depend on any material thing; so that this 'me,' that is to say, the soul by which I am what I am, is entirely distinct from body, and is even more easy to know than is the latter; and even if body were not, the soul would not cease to be what it is. (101)

In current cognitive and neuroscience, however, the cogito is merely an illusion, a concoction of mind that gives shape to the chaos of conscious experience. As this paper argues, O'Rowe's *Terminus* is chiefly the staging of this illusion of consciousness and hence a struggle

---

[11] Mark O'Rowe, *Terminus* (London: Nick Hern Books, 2007), 26. (Further quotations to the text of *Terminus* in this paper refer to this publication and will appear with page number only after relevant quotations).

with the limits of dualistic thinking orientated towards self and soul. The following performance analysis draws from definitions of mind and consciousness from cognitive and neuroscience as well as observations of the play directed by O'Rowe in its premiere run at the Peacock Theatre, Dublin, in 2007.

Mark O'Rowe wrote his first play in the mid 1990s; *The Aspidistra Code*, a play about a young working class Dublin couple who hire a hard man to protect them from a loan shark to whom they are heavily in debt. The setting, characters and violent content of this play heralded the future for the entire of O'Rowe's dramatic oeuvre which is driven primarily by cinema rather than the stage. O'Rowe spent much of his youth watching 'video nasties, cannibal movies and kung-fu flicks' at the local multiplex cinema near his home in Tallaght in the West suburbs of Dublin (Raab 345). At that time the streets and green spaces between many of the the sprawling housing estates of West Dublin were alive with drug dealing, crime and violence. Over the course of the last two decades O'Rowe's writing for stage and screen has vividly captured the layered energies of urban isolation, desperation and aggression. The most successful of his theatre work has been in monologue form, in particular *Howie the Rookie* (1999) and *Terminus* (2007), winning between them a Rooney Prize for Irish Literature, a George Devine Award, an Edinburgh Fringe First, and an Irish Times/ESB Award for Best New Play. In all of this O'Rowe has developed a reputation as a writer who enjoys experimenting with form, who revels in exploring urban violence, and the extremities of darkness and light at the core of human nature. Like no other in Irish theatre O'Rowe's plays place the minutae of everyday urban life against the mythic potential of fantasy and the imagination. His characters are both working class Dubliners and gods from *other* or *under* worlds, heroes and low-lifes, angels and demons.

At the Terminus in the Brain

Terminus consists of a series of alternating monologues delivered by two women and one man, namelessly identified as A, B, and C. The stage setting for the 2007 production is indeterminate and sparse. The play's opening stage direction offers a description of lighting only: '*Lights up on A, B and C. Hold. Lights down on B and C*' (5). Jon Bausor's minimalist setting comprises a giant empty gilt frame which covers the entire vertical circumference of the proscenium arch. Inside this empty frame on the horizontal of the stage floor are three platforms of raised and raked triangular shards of broken glass. The performance opens with the deafening sound of Philip Stewart's sound design of breaking glass as the three cast members – Andrea Irvine (A), Kate Brennan (B), and Aidan Kelly (C) – are revealed beneath Philip Gladwell's sharply defined spotlights. Behind and above the three actors hang shards of broken mirror giving the audience both a rear and frontal view of the actors standing on these individual platforms of glass. The visual impact is more resonant of science fiction fantasy than any named place in Ireland or elsewhere: The three figures hovering in the void of the broken frame could easily be mistaken for the 'teleported' or 'beamed-up' space travellers associated with the Starship Enterprise.

In O'Rowe's combination of urban rap and stream-of-consciousness, meanwhile, these three figures draw the audience into a series of tales of obscene demonic violence that soar from the quotidian into the chimerical. The lion's share of this violence is attributable to the male character, C, whose monologues deliver a litany of spine chilling killings and rapes; acts of such monstrosity that they can only take place within the fictional space of the text and imagination of the audience. As the ultimate psycho killer, C 'hate[s] the world and primarily women' (18). His peculiar addiction to sugary sweets – and primarily Lockets, a brand of honey-filled mint manufactured by the Wrigley confectionary company – is bizarrely incompatible with the sordidness of his repulsive acts and continually pulls the play back to the material world and the physical experience of the character who is speaking. C's first monologue begins in this mode and descends into mayhem:

> I pop a Locket in my mouth, suck, then bite into the shell and – fucking hell! The spill of honey? I *never* fail to find it yummy (14).
>
> ...
>
> Number one, I split from crown to chin. He screams and, relishing the din, I hew number two across the throat and gloat as he gouts arterial spray and flay and, Jaysus, pirouettes as jets of blood arc round him, like some kind of fountain (16).
>
> ...
>
> As I speared her from the rear and, while being fucked, she bucked and brayed, I took my blade and stuck it in, then used my hand to grope about and pull her nethers inside out, and sucked on another Locket, looked as, in time with her death throes, her chest rose and fell – for how long, I couldn't tell – till she was still and honey spilled onto my tongue as I crunched the sweet, got to my feet, headed for the latrine, keen to clean myself of the blood and the gore (18).

As these horrifically visceral stories unfold, significant connections between A, B and C become evident or are implied. A is a retired teacher and part-time Samaritan who goes on the hunt to rescue an ex-pupil called Helen from aborting her unborn child in the final stages in her pregnancy. In the process of this rescue A is reminded of her own estranged daughter who refuses contact following A's jealous seduction of her fiancé. Through common circumstances occurring across the monologues of A and B – a microwaved shepherd's pie on the floor, a shower left running, memories of a girl's night in – it becomes clear that B is this estranged daughter. B lives alone and has difficulty in relationships with the opposite sex. On a night out drinking with friends she is sexually betrayed and ends up on the top of a crane from whence she falls. Before she hits the ground and goes to her death, however, B is scooped up by a demon soul, a creature with a body composed entirely of worms. This demon soul, as quoted in the opening of this paper, has been separated from the host body of C in a bargain that C has made with Satan. The demon soul takes flight with B, they fall in love, make love, and separate. B goes to her death and the soul departs to rejoin C who is on the run following his bloodcurdling killing spree.

On a superficial level the disjointed tales of A, B and C represent the fallout from an increasingly materialistic and secularized world, the alienated, the dysfunctional and the disenfranchised. These are individuals lost in a sea of addiction and obsession, individuals whose only solace lies in a bottomless pit of alcohol, junk-food and one-night-stands. The assignment of alphabetical letters to these beamed-up bodies on stage in contrast to the naming of those about whom they speak points to O'Rowe's deliberate questioning of the existence of character outside of the stories that are told about them. This postmodern device propels the audience not only towards the word but also towards confronting the cogito, the illusion of consciousness as a stable essence located at one precise point in the brain. This also follows on from Elinor Fuchs who has proposed that the character is dead in *Death of Character : Perspectives of Theater After Modernism* (1996). To this effect, there are no characters in *Terminus* in the true sense of the word. There are three actors' bodies in a stage space and images presented through the words of a text.

O'Rowe's alternating monologues make some of the connections between A, B and C tentative and implied rather than solid and explicit, harmonizing form and content in such a way as to reinforce the alienated world in which the characters exist. The text's cinematic imagery and point of view, meanwhile, zooms in and out of the characters' thoughts and actions and in and out of urban or inner city settings; the concrete secular spaces of the dual carriageways, all-night-garages, pubs, cafes, council estates and building sites of Celtic Tiger Ireland. In her first monologue of the play, A lurches from street to taxi to street and in and out of her fleeting thoughts as she makes her way to confront Helen's abortionist lover:

> ... I find a cab to nab and get in and we go, the driver prattling on the way they do. I couldn't be bothered responding. I tune him out and drift and, miffed at my lack of response to his shit, he quits his attempts to engage and sits in a childish rage till we're there and, having paid my fare and got out, I hear, as he pulls away, him say, or rather grunt, 'You ignorant cunt!' and, unfazed by his curse – I know, I know. But I've been called worse – I go to the gate and enter, knock and wait on tenterhooks till she answers the door (8).

Beyond superficial meanings O'Rowe's interplay between text and performance in the 2007 production of *Terminus*, plays with the illusion of consciousness as centrally focused, substantiated and linearly/rationally framed. The stage space in the course of the live performance is literally the terminus of conscious experience; or, to use neuroscientist Antonio Damasio's description of the feeling of consciousness, as a 'movie in the brain' through the mind's eye (*The Feeling of What Happens* 11). To this extent it is no surprise that *Terminus* has been described as a play which takes place either 'inside the heads of his characters' (as described by Garry Hynes in Haughton 159) or inside the heads of its audience. As Laura Collins-Hughes describes the performance of the play in Boston in 2011:

> Fingernails pierce an eyeball and drain it of fluid. A knife slices into a woman while she is having sex. A body implodes beneath the tires of a truck. In Irish playwright Mark O'Rowe's *Terminus*, all of these things happen, but not one of them happens onstage. They occur instead in the minds of the audience, the images painted there by the trio of interwoven monologues that make up the piece.

In her article, 'Performing Power: Violence as Fantasy and Spectacle in Mark O'Rowe's *Made in China* and *Terminus*', Miriam Haughton has persuasively argued that O'Rowe's staging of *Terminus* represents an intent to place emphasis on the 'power of the spoken word while simultaneously denying the expression of the body' (Haughton, 159-160). As she goes on to say, the currency of power within *Terminus* is the delivery of the word and the gaze operating between performer and audience. In the course of performing their overlapping monologues the three stationary figures do not interact with each other. Instead, they engage face-to-face with the audience, confiding in them, sometimes posing direct questions and assuming answers on the audience's behalf. Midway through her first monologue, for instance, A asks the audience, 'Did I mention, by the way ...? Okay. But did I also say ...' (6). Later on she says, 'Bear with me, though, and entertain any crying I might do, and I'll try my best to explain ...' (21). In the protocol of theatre attendance the audience is trapped in its seated position, unable to disengage from the powerful exchange that takes place in the course of the performance. By gazing directly at the audience the actors share the same space of *being* with them in the moment of performance. Their lack of action and their obviously theatrical setting does not allow them to merely *seem to be* and hence they must *seem* and *be* in that shared moment between auditorium and stage. Audience and actor are thus present to each other in the moment of consciousness and in this feeling of being, to borrow Damasio's words again, 'at the movies in the brain' through the 'mind's eye.'

In investigating the performance moment and the dynamic between audience and stage Bruce McConachie has adopted a cognitive linguisitic approach which is useful in the analysis of the performance of O'Rowe's *Terminus*. According to McConachie the 'conceptual blending' theories of Gilles Fauconnier and Mark Turner propose that our assimilation of performance involves the amalgamation of stimulii and mental spaces. We blend the content of more than one space to arrive at a new blended space that contains the compressed contents of the former. When we watch an actor in performance we watch (the actor's skill) from the outside, but also feel ourselves to be with/in the performance, feeling what the performer-in-role is feeling. We can only achieve conceptual blending as body-minds, however, alive to thought, sensory perception, feelings and emotions (McConachie 553-577). The vocal sounds of *Terminus* facilitate such blending in their sensory onomatopoeic impact. O'Rowe's words aurally link body and mind, thought and sensation:

> So, I turn with a wobble, hobble toward the gate, get through it. My dinner leaps up into my throat and I spew it, dousing the street, hearing the sound of retreating laughter, a door closing after (9).

In its interplay between text and performance the 2007 production of *Terminus* pushes the audience into the terminus of the brain confronting head on the deceptive illusion of consciousness as substantiated, linearly and rationally framed and centrally focused. The clean lines of the minimalist setting may be said to suggest a parallel with Descartes' definition of consciousness, which provides a rational framing or shape to space and awareness. This is incompatible, however, with our actual experience of what it is like to be in the world at any given moment in time. The busyness of *Terminus's* fragmented monologues and their imagistic content conflict with Bausor's visually clean lines, bringing the audience up close to the staging or ordering of conscious experience. The setting and the soundscape's earth shattering announcement of the breaking mirror resists the fourth wall and reinforces the play's attempt to disrupt illusory perceptions of reality. The contrast between the minimalistic setting of the performance and the busyness of the text, meanwhile, throws emphasis onto the words spoken by the actors on stage. *Terminus* in this regard is the staging of the experiences of A, B and C as they come to consciousness in the moment of performance. This is further enabled by the text's positioning in a continual rambling present tense, in its attendance to the minutiae of each and every detail of the speaker's experiences, bringing what would otherwise be regarded as inconsequential into the frame of performance. The sensory atmosphere of a physical environment not present on stage is unravelled via the rhythms of the text in tune with its content which hypnotically draws the listener in. With B we:

> [...] meander the minute or so to McGurk's; sink one, sink two, then bid adieu to the barman – his reply to me each and every time, 'God bless' – depart then, head to the M&S, my dinner to purchase, my day-to-day to adhere to, near to identical all, said days, near rote, you know? Near reflex now.
>
> The bus home then, the silent flat. No cat nor any kind of pet. The sofa – sit. The telly – hit the remote. Reward – the illusion of presence through voices (10).

At the terminus in the brain we are brought into contact with another violent reality that parallels the violence contained in the stories told by A, B and C. In bringing this feeling to the fore *Terminus* wrenches apart any singular view of reality in its alternating monologue form which, like the cinema, allows O'Rowe to imaginatively compress or make leaps from one time and space to another, and from one perspective to another. According to cognitive scientist, Daniel Dennett consciousness is not a single picture but an image that we ourselves produce. In *Consciousness Explained* Dennett explains that the phenomenological truth is the truth experienced by the subject that is not always true. Speaking of phenomenal space, he says 'This is a space into which or in which nothing is literally projected; its properties are simply constituted by the beliefs of the (heterophenomenological) subject" (131). 'The idea of a special center in the brain,' he says, 'is the most tenacious bad idea bedeviling our attempt to think about consciousness' (108). Theorizing against Cartesian dualism, Dennett suggests that consciousness is more a series of processes of 'multiple drafts' or 'fragments at various stages of editing in various places in the brain' (113). To put it another way, consciousness does not have a centre and is not a singular process; our single picture of reality, our Cartesian view exists only because we create it. Akin to Dennett's 'multiple drafts at various stages of editing', events within the three separate monologues of *Terminus* occur simultaneously and come together at the conclusion of the play. The speakers, meanwhile, are continually checking themselves and their stories as they go along. Midway through her first monologue, for instance, A asks the audience, 'Did I mention, by the way ...? Okay. But did I also say ...? I didn't.' (6). And more expansively later on:

> After a certain length of time, some associations occur in my mind. I'm comparing Helen and her mother, you see, their falling out, to my daughter and me, our own separation, brought about by ...
> That's a glaring omission.
> Shit.
> That's right. I've a child of my own. 'A child!' (21).

Flitting here and there, forwards and backwards, the three monologues provide the audience with a fragmented disorientating experience, pushing against the impulse of coherence and continually forcing us towards the 'movie in the brain' through the 'mind's eye'.

Illusions of Consciousness

According to film maker David Cronenberg, at the root of all horror films is the Cartesian split; the terror of mind and body separating at the point of death. According to Steven Taylor

> Cronenberg has stressed his fascination with Cartesian dualism in statements too numerous to mention. He envisions the ultimate comment on this unfathomable 'split' (and the basis of all horror) as being the process of physical death. 'Why should a healthy mind die, just because the body is not healthy? ... There seems to be something wrong with that. It's very easy to see why many philosophers detach the mind from the body ... But I don't believe that.' It is this anguish of contradiction that lies at the heart of the painful mystery in his films. Cronenberg sees an apparent split—but his intuitions deny that such a thing exists.

O'Rowe's *Terminus* is poised on the brink of this terror exposing a search for alternatives and a longing for the self to be rescued from death at the point of this assumed separation. When B is rescued by the demon soul as she falls from the crane her onlookers are transfixed by the sight of the demon and the possibility of 'a death deferred':

> Then there's the creature's hooves, its horns, all these things composed of worms as well; its tail, its prick – it's male – their slick, fat interwoven shapes, like spiderweb or scaffolding, or a machine whose purpose is to power the creature – and me in his arms – up higher past my betrayers, who gape in wonder at a death deferred by the timely intervention ... of, unless I'm mistaken ... a demon (14).

While drowning later in the play, however, B reveals her attempt to hold on to her 'self' in the the process of dying:

> I try to reclaim my waning name in vain – it's gone – or where I'm from – that too – the who and the why, the I; all fly from my mind till I just kind of am, then. [...] Bam! (45).

The culminating monologues further extend this preoccupation of the play by insinuating a fatalistic loop of reincarnation between the stories of A, B, and C. Helen, the young woman who has been rescued from her abortionist/lover by A, dies when she is knocked down by a truck driven by C. Helen's baby is born at the scene of the accident, survives, and is handed over to A who speaks into the ear of the newly born baby, but her words are only hinted at in the overlapping structure of the play. As they appear between the concluding monologues of A and B, the words delivered by A, 'You'll have to be strong from here' (45) could have several meanings: A's thoughts as she stands at the door of her estranged daughter's flat hoping for a reunion, A's message to the baby she holds before she hands it back to the paramedic, A's message to B while she enters the reincarnated body of the new-born baby. The latter is inferred by A's words and the placement of the line at the end of B's monologue in which she describes the moment of her death:

> ... a rent in my sunless sphere appears, lets in the light that sears my eyes, I shut them tight and feel myself lifted from hot to cold, enfolded in something soft and borne aloft, the waft of many smells assailing me, the ability to identify them failing me; the wind, the clamour, hammering in my ears, this fearsome fusion of sounds into which I've been cast and to which, at last, I open my eyes to see, through the glare, the face of a woman, streaked with tears – I'm back in the world, it appears – and, she's smiling down at me like you would at a child, her expression melancholy yet

> beguiled, and, though I don't know her at all, she evokes in me such love, I bawl, appalled as I am by the idea that she's about to abandon me, to disappear, a fear borne out when after a minute she puts her mouth to my ear and, in it whispers words I'm unable to decode (45).

At the moment of death B is unable to identify the woman or to decode the words uttered into her ear. The links between baby, A and B are thus tenuous and conjectural. These hinted at entanglements with reincarnation and fate resist closure and leave openings for the process of imagining. In this way O'Rowe's stage space struggles with and is inconclusive in considering alternatives to the belief in soul and life after death.

As outlined in the first section of this paper, Haughton has addressed the complex questions of power, myth, and violence in the performance of *Terminus* forming the view that this play

> suggests the increasingly fragmentary nature of social living, with instances of isolation and despair provoking and facilitating a culture of crisis, manifest as violent exchanges, in a place caught between various worlds of myth, story and cultural despair (155).

Terminus, she suggests, disproves the Foucaultian belief in the restricted movement of the social body. 'In these fantasies', she suggests 'there are no restrictions or restraint on physical exchange with the body' (Haughton, 156). Nevertheless, '[v]iolence as a punitive measure and violence as a currency to display personal status in this linguistically coded construct of Dublin are apparent' (Haughton, 158). My arguments here complement Haughton's views and observations by paring back the philosophical frame of *Terminus* to the core of O'Rowe's dramaturgy. In this regard I argue that this dramaturgy attests to a more fundamental creative inquisitiveness about the chaos and fragmentation of conscious experience, and that the violence at the centre of the play's content is paralleled by the violence of the performance of O'Rowe's monologue form which tears into the illusion of consciousness and self. The play chronicles a struggle with the limits of dualistic experience. A, B and C are body-minds obsessed with the physical world in which they exist, their appetites, pleasures and pains. In the play there is nothing lofty or noble about mind or soul and O'Rowe does not shy away from the unsavoury details of the body; the bad breath, the spit, the vomit, the snot. In *Terminus* a fear of the Cartesian split might be elevated to the level of myth, but mind and body are firmly located in the physical present on stage in the delivery of performance echoing Damasio's claim that

> It is not only the separation between mind and brain that is mythical: the separation between mind and body is probably just as fictional. The mind is *embodied*, in the full sense of the term, not just *embrained*. (*Descartes Error* 118)

From a political standpoint Cartesianism supports the privileging of mind over body and the Judeo Christian belief in an inner spirit or soul which continues to exist after the death of the physical body. In an uncertain world the idea of a transcendent soul is a tempting lifeline, a possible rescue in the face of the certainty of death. Cartesianism is the foundation of Enlightenment rationality and dualistic thinking which separates, splits and alienates through oppositional thinking, territorializing space and segregating identity. William Demastes traces developments in drama and theatre which correspond to developments in theories of mind, highlighting the significance of such theories in the politics of performance. Forms of theatre which pivot around a Cartesian central character with its stable ego, for instance, cloak hegemonic ideas of identity and assume closed worlds of cause and effect and either/or situations that trap their characters within them. As Dennett and others have claimed, however, consciousness is a dynamic continual process that never reaches a destination but feeds back into itself, adjusting and achieving awareness at countless points along its neural progress. This definition parallels the conditions of postmodern and postdramatic theatres which eschew character and linear narrative, destabilizing and disorientating their audiences who are not allowed to sink back into the darkness of the auditorium. Under such conditions actors are carriers of the text, and stage action involves simultaneity and multi-dimensionality. In such theatre, therefore, the illusion of consciousness, as William Demastes says, is 'staged not as some discrete, autonomous entity, rather we are seeing full efforts of bridging the very mind-body chasm that the new scientists have been attempting' (24). In such theatre the Cartesian experience is confronted and falsified through the bridging of mind and body, the notion of character as essence is challenged, and the hegemonic deliberately resisted.

The material presence of C's demon in *Terminus* refutes Descartes' definition of consciousness as a soul capable of existing beyond the body and the material world. The demon is physically grounded and interacts with B and C. As C describes the demon towards the end of the play 'its form, composed as it is of a hundred thousand worms, its size, is someone I recognize: myself, or rather, my other half' (48). According to Neuroscientist, Antonio Damasio, 'soul and spirit, with all their dignity and human scale, are now complex and unique states of an organism' *(Descartes Error* 252). In other words, our souls and demons are states of ourselves that live and die with us as organisms. Like the worms which make up the body of the demon in *Terminus* we are no more than a network of chemical and cellular interactions which the brain cannot resist giving shape to in a propensity towards substantiating consciousness.

In 2001, not long after the success of *Howie the Rookie*, O'Rowe claimed that he wanted to 'push Irish theatre on to the next level' (in conversation with Gerard Stembridge). As Clare Wallace points out the monologue form solicits 'questions about the very nature of theatre itself, about the nature of performative and audience response, truth and illusion, narrative and experience' (6). In *Terminus* it appears that O'Rowe is experimenting with monologue in order to explore the illusion of consciousness, returning to an archaic form of storytelling as a means of dealing with questions about the dominance of the word. A cognitive scientific approach to the entire range of monologue forms has yet to be fully undertaken, however, and until such time we await a true understanding of what Mark O'Rowe's *Terminus* has to offer.

Works Cited:

Performance:
Terminus (Peacock Theatre, 2007), written and directed by Mark O'Rowe, lighting by Philip Gladwell, sound by Philip Stewart with cast including: Andrea Irvine (A), Kate Brennan (B), Aidan Kelly (C)

Primary Text:
O'Rowe, Mark, *Terminus* (London: Nick Hern Books, 2007)

Secondary Texts:
Collins-Hughes, Laura, 'Grisly Scenes in the Mind's Eye, *The Boston Globe*, 4th February 2011.

Damasio, Antonio, *Descartes Error: Emotion, Reason, and the Human Brain* (New York: Penguin Books, 1994)

Damasio, Antonio, *The Feeling of What Happens: Body and Emotion in the Making of Consciousness* (New York: Harcourt Inc, 1999)

Demastes, William, W., *Staging Consciousness: Theater and the Materialization of Mind* (Ann Arbor: University of Michigan Press, 2002)

Dennett, Daniel, *Consciousness Explained* (London: Allen Lane, 1991)

Descartes, René, *The Philosophical Works of Descartes, rendered into English by Elizabeth S. Haldane and G.R.T. Ross*, Vol. 1 (New York: Cambridge University Press, 1970)

Fuchs, Elinor. *Death of Character : Perspectives of Theater After Modernism* (Bloomington and Indianapolis: Indiana University Press, 1996).

Haughton, Miriam, 'Performing Power: Violence as Fantasy and Spectacle in Mark O'Rowe's *Made in China* and *Terminus*' (*New Theatre Quarterly*, 2011), 153-166

McConachie, Bruce, 'Falsifiable Theories for Theatre and Performance Studies' *Theatre Journal*, Vol. 59, No. 4, Dec 2007

O'Rowe, Mark. In conversation with Gerard Stembridge, (NAYD) 9 February 2001.

Raab, Michael, *The Methuen Drama Guide to Contemporary Irish Playwrights* eds Martin Middeke and Peter Paul Schnierer (London: Methuen, 2010), 345-364

Taylor, Steven, (Gyrus), Psychoplasmics *Body Mutation and Disease in the Films of David Cronenberg* http://dreamflesh.com/essays/psychoplasmics/

Wallace, Clare, 'Monologue Theatre, Solo Performance and Self as Spectacle' in Clare Wallace, ed. *Monologues: Theatre, Performance, Subjectivity* (Prague: Litteraria Pragensia, 2006), 1-17

9 | Interwoven Locality and a Globalized Dublin in Mark O'Rowe's *Terminus*

Nelson Barre

The world is shrinking. In every corner of the world, the spread of technology has made culture, place, and identity subjects of contested definition. Sociologists and critical theorists have long posited that border-crossing interconnectivity makes every country available to international participation and influence. Chief among these forces is the idea of globalization, a term with as many definitions as there are critics discussing its expansive concepts of the world at large. Art and other cultural expressions have thus taken approaches to displaying this notion of interrelated themes, stories, and people and placing them on a global stage. Quite literally, it is within this context Irish playwright Mark O'Rowe has situated his works. In *Terminus*, O'Rowe exhibits an understanding of Dublin as contemporary and globalized even as stereotypes of Irish pastoralism continue to abound. Today's Ireland is a modern culture with deep connections not only abroad but within its own communities. The play creates tensions between globalized misconceptions about major cities, cultural versus personal morality, and divergences from cultural stereotypes. These questions are impossible to quantify at a global level, but O'Rowe provides a framework in which an analysis of human interdependency begins to flourish. *Terminus* displays globalization as a force with positive outcomes. Characters experience isolation, embrace mobility, and engage with moral quandaries as a means of achieving connections to the world around them. Instead of focusing on an ever-shrinking world that threatens to erase individuals, the figures that inhabit O'Rowe's world confront their solitude and transcend it as they find hope in relationships where once previously they saw only desperation. This essay presents a new discourse surrounding *Terminus*, one which questions previous discussions not only of the play but of the global context with which it interacts.

Many critical responses to O'Rowe's work highlight the violence and often abrasive elements in his storytelling (Raab; Haughton). Among the reviews of his plays, critics have been quick to label his voice as poetic yet morally askew (Singleton; Collins-Hughes). The playwright embraces this attitude toward his work, stating that he was always more of a kung-fu film fan than a theatre-goer (Zinoman). As such, he has admitted that the first scene he often envisions for his writing stems from sex or violence. As a result, many writers focus almost exclusively on the savagery within his fictional worlds. The playwright's first major success, *Howie the Rookie* (1999), ends with a narrated fight sequence detailing every broken bone, every lost ounce of bodily fluid, and ends when one of the two protagonists is thrown from a window and impaled on a fence. The audience, however, is spared the visual torment of seeing this enacted onstage as the play is told entirely through monologue. O'Rowe's next play, *Made in China* (2001), did not offer such a reprieve. Instead the play's climax displays the brutalizing of three characters onstage. Critics have cited this play as pure sensationalism, an attempt to push the boundaries of audience tolerance within the medium of live performance. It can also be argued that these two plays comment on the sensory numbing associated with violence in the contemporary media. These claims have led to much criticism of Irish playwrights in general as excessively violent, even in the waning popularity of British In-Yer-Face theatre (Raab; Logan). Even *Terminus* (2007) has been often decried as an excuse for excessive brutality. *Terminus* does, however, embody a return to the monologue format which does not present actions during the performance. Instead it is left to the audience to form their own visions of the atrocities which befall the characters.

But these tales imply more than a fascination with violence; O'Rowe's works all rely on the trend of globalization and international interconnectivity. Reconsidering definitions of globalization provides the basis for this analysis of *Terminus*. Theorists often describe the term as an expansion of the world and its interlinking consciousness while also noting the shrinking effect it seems to invoke. In his seminal study on the subject, Roland Robertson defines globalization 'as a concept [that] refers both to the compression of the world and the intensification of consciousness of the world as a whole' (Robertson 9).

This duality often leads to the use of subsections, which will usually include some mixture of spreading culture(s), capitalism/branding, and the influences these have on the world at large versus the individual. This essay explores each of these aspects with an emphasis on the latter – the idea that each person exists as their own entity but also as part of a larger whole. Therefore, it is important to note that when using the term 'globalization,' it is not solely in reference to the idea that cultures are becoming homogenized but rather that they are a complex mixture of past and present, and cultures near and far. Each of these aspects works within my definition of globalization which describes the world as an array of individual expressions, each of which seeks a connection with others and is made more complex by this process. That is not to say that entities within this global, technological, cultural development do not understand their place beyond themselves. Each character in *Terminus* desperately wants to increase their connections to others because the world seems so vast, dark, and oppressive. In this way, O'Rowe's play shows that advances in communication and travel combine with international marketing to serve as vehicles for connecting people across oceans as much as cities or even neighbourhoods.

In particular among O'Rowe's works, *Terminus* presents the most interweaved stories as the three-part monologue format simultaneously allows the characters to travel anywhere through lyrical description while also physically limiting the actual movement and action of the actors onstage. The original production utilized sparse staging to highlight the storytelling and importance of each individual narrative. The actors' perpetual presence provided a reminder of their presence in the performance space and in the world at large. In short, the story follows three marginalized entities in Dublin: A, an older suicide call-centre worker and former secondary school teacher; B, a young woman stuck in the routine of daily life and A's estranged daughter; and C, a man who sold his soul to the Devil for a beautiful singing voice to overcome his crippling shyness, but by a clever trick of contractual wording is left voiceless when performing in front of crowds. The characters each begin their tale with a lamentation – a lack of human connection in a world that only provides the illusion of companionship. As the stories progress, however, their connections become apparent even in the alleged anonymity of Ireland's largest city. A tries to save her former student, Helen, from aborting her child and from the actions of Celine, a woman intent on abusing the entirety of Dublin. A successfully rescues the pregnant woman but only to lose her as C crashes through the city in a truck. B goes out with friends but is betrayed as she falls from a crane. Instead of death she is caught mid-air by a demon made of worms, C's soul who has come to reclaim his body. The worm demon and B create a relationship, but it is short-lived as angels set wrongs right and lead B to her death. After dying, however, B returns to the world of the living as the newborn child of A's former student. This moment connects the mother and daughter one last time. C tries to overcome his timidity, but instead has taken the injustice done upon him by Satan as a personal affront and a reason to punish the world for its refusal to accept him. C seduces women and mid-coitus murders them. His crimes are broadcast via radio and he must flee, which leads to his running down Helen in a truck. C's soul does catch him and disembowels him from the same crane where B fell. In his final moments, C is able to overcome his fear of performing as a crowd gathers and listens to him sing Bette Midler's 'Wind Beneath My Wings.' This is O'Rowe's most fantastical world, and it provides him with the necessary latitude to explore globalization as a means for creating hope and connection, even in a world built on moral ambiguities, international commodities and seeming detachment.

While this may not seem like the equation for an international hit, one need look no further than Broadway, one year before O'Rowe's play premiered, to the wildly successful production of Brian Friel's *Faith Healer* starring Ralph Fiennes. This is not to say that *Terminus* was meant for Broadway, but the success of Irish monologue plays by writers such as Conor McPherson and Friel had already attested to the international popularity of the form. The monologue play is built on the global model. This form expects spectators to utilize the skills of a contemporary citizen: compress information, summarize, and assess. As Patrick Lonergan argues in *Theatre and Globalization*, 'An audience member at a monologue play must therefore receive information, process it, evaluate it, and compare it with information already received' (183). He explains further that the form relies on compression not only of a large amount of material into a single voice but also on the reduction of action and space to the confinement of the theatre and imagination. The monologue places responsibility for interpretation with the audience and relies on the competence of viewers to receive the actors' words.

As such, the brand and product was primed for global success even with its dark content. This type of information reception suits contemporary eyes and ears and has made it even more accessible to international audiences. Nicholas Grene argues, 'Irish drama is outward-directed, created as much to be viewed from outside as from inside Ireland' (3). Acknowledgement of global presence is important for considering thematic tenets of contemporary Irish art. Throughout its history, theatre (especially the Irish variety) was utilized as a product which could be created and sold across borders. *Terminus* exemplifies this commodification as it toured to America, England, and Australia. Among many initiatives to dispense Irish arts overseas, Culture Ireland and Imagine Ireland were instrumental in bringing O'Rowe's piece to international audiences. The touring production, whose cast appears on the Abbey Theatre's published text of the play, commanded sell-out performances and was variously lauded as a 'feat of storytelling' (Logan) and exhibits the 'very particular, intrinsically Irish writing style of Mark O'Rowe, who shows himself to be no less than a 21st-century Shakespeare' (Syke). These monikers produce a feeling that Ireland produces art that is suited both to local and international consumption. Reviewers recognize the work's Irishness but fail to note the global implications of a successful touring production.

In the same way *Terminus* reminds us that people are not always aware of their connections to others – even if they share common locales or interests. For example, A and B have been estranged for years but are, in the final moments of their respective stories, reunited because of C's rampage through Dublin. These connections are part of the globalized experience. Beyond the notion of the 'butterfly effect' (a butterfly beat its wings in the prehistoric era which sets a hurricane in 2005 in motion), O'Rowe's play seems to advocate that people in contemporary societies want to connect on a more basic level. From the play's outset, A eulogizes her experience as a Samaritans' suicide call-centre operator saying: 'fearing I don't have the sand, the grit, the bit of detachment required – Ah, shit – Sure, mired as I am in sympathy, you see, what possible help can I be to these loveless lost, what cost to them my hapless, helpless, hopeless best, my messed-up endeavours?' (5). Here, A shows her misgivings about connections in a technological age. She is distanced from the people because of the telephone, but this is her only means of supporting them. In addition, she finds difficulty providing what she feels would constitute real help because of this detachment. A has joined the ranks of a call-centre community, but there is no mention of co-workers. She reaches out to people beyond her immediate world. Her desire to provide support seems to stem from her feelings of guilt after betraying her daughter years earlier when she slept with B's then-fiancé. But this only reinforces her own life of solitude, as she refuses conversation with bartenders, taxi drivers, or other Dubliners in hopes that she can embody the role of 'mother' by saving a person's life. A has fallen victim to the modern age of globalization in as much as she is unable to look locally for comfort and instead must use technology to expand her influence, providing her with a false sense of satisfaction.

But this situation is not unique. As B takes up her story, we realize that she is also mired in a world which consistently reinforces a person's isolation. She describes her routine as 'day-to-day to adhere to, near to identical all, said days, near rote, you know? Near reflex now ... The bus home then, the silent flat. No cat nor any kind of pet. The sofa – sit. The telly – hit the remote. Reward – the illusion of presence through voices' (10). B has nothing but the monotony of repetition. She recognizes the television as an imposter for human contact, an illusion of the modern world for interaction with others. Easy access to technology and the proliferation of images provide stimuli, but individuals recognize the false sense of security and connection they provide. In a bout of frustration, B goes out with friends – a couple, Lenny and Lee, and a single friend, Andy – in hopes of moving beyond this loneliness, only to have her reason for disconnection confirmed; the friends betray her. After a few drinks, they climb a crane and Lee seduces Andy, allowing Lenny to approach B ultimately causing her fall. Even before B recognizes their duplicity, the young woman notes the seemingly faceless masses of people who appear 'exiled and aimless' (12). These words describe a tendency in today's world more than the people themselves. If O'Rowe had chosen to follow any number of other Dubliners, the story would have been markedly different but would have portrayed a similarly unique tale about people's solitude in a quickly globalizing world. B recognizes this and actively seeks to refute it, only to have the faces around her obscured by the anonymity of the city's expansiveness.

The most pronounced example of isolation appears in C's story. He narrates his outing to a singles' event, hoping to overcome his crippling shyness and find a woman with whom he can dance. He has set his standards and expectations low, as one might do after years of rejection (not only by women but society as well). But he is not alone in this cloud of dismissal, as his date confides 'how forsaken one can feel sometimes, how left behind. And I find myself agreeing, seeing I'm in the selfsame boat, you know? The both of us solitary, pathetic and lonely, only not tonight' (15). The contemporary world may appear to be more interconnected than ever, but for these characters it has been nothing more than a proliferation of missed opportunities. These lamentations portray a world that seems to exemplify global interrelations which in fact emphasizes a lack of intimate relationships at the expense of spreading influence and technology. C commiserates with these sentiments, but that does not change his feeling that the world at large has actively shunned him. One could argue that this shows C's immaturity and inability to move beyond a perceived slight against him for an embarrassing night of failed karaoke, but that in turn fails to note the endemic attitude that this desire for connection is a basic human need. His deep dissatisfaction becomes more than an overreaction to a small problem. Rather C's detachment from society portrays an extreme response to a lack of respect and acceptance. Each of these three characters lives a solitary existence filled with the illusion of interaction. They all battle their misgivings about how they (do not) fit into society, and this fight against loneliness proves to be the main objective in the play.

The characters try to refuse their isolation by rejecting values which have placed each of them where they are. Among the many effects of the postmodern era on globalization is this challenge to how people are expected to exist within society. This becomes particularly troubling when considering the influences of world-wide standards of morality and their fluid nature. Mike Featherstone, in his book *Undoing Culture*, discusses at length the deconstruction of the West's ideologies in the postmodern era. On the subject of shifting social convention, he says: '[T]he changing global circumstance as a result of the process of globalization has provoked a particular Western reaction to this situation in the form of postmodernism, which has engaged in a far-reaching questioning of its own tradition' (12). In this way, contemporary society diverges from previous modes of communication and levels of meaning. The isolated characters of *Terminus* live within a quickly changing realm of questionable decision-making, but that seems to be the norm for contemporary Irish playwrighting. O'Rowe breaks expectations of characters with whom audiences should empathize. C has reason to be upset about his treatment by society's privileged few who are able to interact and mingle without any difficulty. C takes matters into his own hands when he is heckled by men outside the bar when he leaves with the woman. He returns later to exact vengeance (per his violent streak) via a balletic slicing of the attackers. It is difficult to cheer for this man whose actions are psychopathic, and yet he stands for certain principles and refuses to allow people free reign in verbally abusing others. He actively works against the expectation that any person can mistreat someone and get away with it. Instead, he takes a vigilante approach against these thugs in defence of his latest victim (the irony of murder ending her suffering and retaliating against those who caused it). The complexity of the situation troubles an audience's feelings about C. Is there any sympathy to be had for someone who so attacks others? Or is it the lingering effect of society's cruelty toward his introversion compounded by Satan's Faustian bargain? Instead of clear answers, O'Rowe seems to revel in the ambiguity displayed by his characters. The play denies that characters with easily grasped moral centres reside in the contemporary world.

On the other hand, B seems the most sympathetic and straightforward because of her innocence among Dublin's other denizens. While it may seem contradictory to describe people as both individual and part of the masses, this duality proves to be integral to O'Rowe's construction of this world. B describes her naïveté at going along with her friend, who provided her own boyfriend the opportunity to have a sexual encounter with the trusting young woman. When B relates this part of the tale to C's soul, she receives support but is quickly denied real comfort because of the pursuing angels – 'from Heaven, and they're the ones given the task of setting wrong things right' (28). This presents a dilemma for audiences who encounter the tale. Some may condemn the young woman for making poor choices but few would say she deserved to die for her decisions. The global shifting of moralities may seem to have little effect in this instance, but it is because of outside forces that B was led into this situation. She only recognizes the treachery against her as its symptom when it is too late. B describes her supposed friends, noting that she should have seen this coming. While most people might be reviled by these actions, this type of situation seems to be the rule rather than the exception. The focus on individual expectations leads to selfish decisions. This is a moralistic generalization and obviously would not apply to Dublin as a whole, much less the entire world, but O'Rowe seems intent on showing that people have this capacity. Contemporary society seems to encourage these types of duplicitous actions which provide self-satisfaction above more magnanimous decisions. Especially with the dominance of global capitalism, not only economically but personally people are encouraged to make choices that will benefit themselves. Even when this is clearly damaging to someone else, cultures still promote the negative aspects of globalization by not punishing those who do wrong but the opposite.

An equally difficult conundrum of morality appears as A continues her story, detailing her pursuit of Helen. A receives the call while working at Samaritans only to realize her former student is in serious danger at the hands of Celine, a woman who makes even groups of street-tough men stand aside when she passes. But A continues to think of Helen, allowing her emotions to come into play. She describes the

> sudden fit of guilt I feel since her call, the shame, for never having intervened at the time, combined with the fact it was me she got back there tonight, my line, is beginning to feel like a sign, a dare, or a command, to find her, and I understand if you deem this kind of reasoning extreme, but I've always been a woman who'll embrace her intuition and obey it, and today it's saying, Save this girl. (6)

This response seems like one with which an audience would agree and support. But A still recognizes the difficulty in choosing to do the right thing. She sees this attempt to help another person as 'extreme,' something out of the ordinary for modern life. In the introduction to a collection of his plays, Irish playwright Tom Murphy argues that 'Love, tenderness, loyalty, generosity go out the door in the struggle for survival' (Murphy *xi*). O'Rowe echoes and revises the dramaturgy of an earlier Irish dramatist who highlights the brutality of human interactions. Characters in *Terminus* form their identities based on assumptions of safety and continued existence. Often when there is the fear of harm, an individual will resist the urge to intervene. Morals are outweighed by the need for personal survival. This becomes part of the social landscape, as has been seen in B and C's respective stories. According to evolutionary psychologists, people choose selfishness, actively rejecting human connection, and this is part of the evolution of global cultures (Dawkins, Wright). But even among the fear of harm to oneself, A and B choose to act which provides a glimmer of hope among the violence and perfidy which surround them.

But is this ambivalence the fault of humanity, or part of globalization? Social commentators have long deplored the technological movement of the world, often citing limited face-to-face interactions in favour of digital communication (Derrida 373). While this is valid, it is important to note that these also enhance the ability to connect. Media, telephones, and vehicles have all become part of the social evolution of humanity in the past decades at this exponentially increased rate. In the play, the characters experience a steady movement which brings them away from the centre only to place them on a collision course. For example, A mobilizes herself as she pursues her former student and her assailant. Most frequently she travels by foot, but her use of taxis, the Dublin Area Rapid Transit (DART), and telephones gives her not only the ability to continue her quest but also the chance to traverse boundaries of culture. She sidesteps drunkards and thugs, witnesses violence against passersby, and enters neighbourhoods she would otherwise avoid; A experiences the city through intimate exploration, which is integral to globalization as much as international travel and media. As stated earlier, these individual experiences provide a type of interconnectivity that otherwise would be ignored. People who live in a certain part of town are often happy to stay within their routine, ignoring or actively evading specific areas populated by unsavoury sorts. While this attempt at separation is not a recent development, the argument for globalization tries to undermine the evasion and show interconnections via travel. A moves beyond these expected limitations, exercising a freedom of movement that would have been unheard of prior to the contemporary age.

But B is not the only one to utilize transportation; C takes control of various vehicles as well, and travels quite a distance even moving beyond the confines of the city. It is important to note that he finds Dublin to be both his freedom and confinement. The population torments him through its rejection (not to mention pursuit by authorities), so he must flee. But once he leaves the metropolitan area, a deep unease consumes him. C laments the absence of people saying, '[I]t isn't long before my good cheer disappears, and hunger and fears of being lost accost me. Field to field, my travels fail to yield any sign of civilization, just this proliferation of green, these gates to climb, this uneven terrain to traverse, this merciless cold, this fatigue, this league of griefs' (33). Outside Dublin, a person is exposed to the elements and lack of civilization – contemporary comforts. C longs to 'disappear back into that big concealing town,' a place where he feels more at ease because amongst others, he can fade into the masses. His recognition of the city as a place that both conceals and exposes is telling for the understanding of globalization. The complexity continues to multiply as opinions of certain spaces and places shift based on the circumstances of an individual's experience. But this duality stems from the ease with which a person might navigate a city, county, or country.

Technology proves to work both ways as his description is provided via radio transmission and C is recognized, leading him to crash his vehicle in an attempt to escape. Information today travels faster than any other commodity. As such, it becomes clear that C cannot escape into anonymity (which ironically is exactly what he desires, even as he craves recognition for his singing ability) by leaving the city. Instead he must return to Dublin, which will conceal him. In a world that claims interconnectivity at levels never before achieved, it is almost antithetical to believe someone might escape into the very place where people are most connected. And yet, this refers back to B's feeling of routine and solitude – most people would ignore someone they pass on the street. Or as in A's case, it seems extraordinary that a person would be willing to sacrifice their own desires in service of someone else. If a person wants to withdraw, they can do so more easily in the crush of the city as opposed to a small village. This understanding of globalized society is what drives C back to civilization and also what keeps him alone and unhappy.

In contrast to this complex desire for both obscurity and societal approval, B moves beyond her comfortable routine in an attempt to find a purpose. Instead, as stated earlier, she finds that she cannot trust people. Once she is saved by C's soul, however, she finds a new desire for connection. B listens to the worm demon's similar story of betrayal, being sold to the Devil for a voice, and they experience a connection built on trust and tenderness. But like C, the pair must still travel great distances to escape the authority of angels who come to end her life. This question returns to the debate on morality, except this time the ambiguity rests with entities who are deified for their goodness. Instead of allowing this young woman to continue her life, angels are the unswerving arbiters of a stunted moral code. C's soul rejects this and their bond grows stronger as they travel through the air, into the earth, and back above ground to escape her fate. The distance and intimacy of travel leads to a deeper connection which would have never existed otherwise. The young woman describes the night's importance saying: 'My short-lived love who prolonged my life so that I might, at the end, understand a love that goes beyond any I've ever known before; a love that, though doomed, is truly pure' (42). B's mobility between her near-death and actual death provides her with the brief glimpse of a real connection. Flight has allowed the pair to escape from the limitations of life, but for only so long. The unlikely romance ends as the angels claim B and bring her extended life to an end. Her desire to escape fate could not be avoided, even with the ability to move free of the confines of society. It seems the mobility provided a moment of relief only to take it away, which shows a darker side to movement in a globalized world. The ability to travel quickly is often lauded, but the complexity it creates among authority figures furthers the assumption that it should always fall under control and rules. Masao Miyoshi posits that, 'we are heading toward a future where the pace of change will accelerate to such an extent that the trace of history may be erased as time hurries along through our everyday life' (19). The current magnitude of communication and the accelerated travel of information has become a burden that denies relationships. The unprecedented speed is terrifying and threatens to destroy history itself. But globalization, in my understanding, is about breaking that relationship down, and showing the necessity for interconnectivity. The characters of *Terminus* transform this pace into something meaningful and appropriate to individual experience.

O'Rowe's world maintains a level of reality while also pushing beyond these boundaries. The limitations of human existence are enough that this should be the end of B's story. As she drowns in the waters of the River Liffey, memories wash over her and then disappear. Similar to a person who might encounter news or information through various media, B only glimpses these moments of her life. This same desensitization to knowledge and its acquirement occur every second in today's world. People have access to various media which instantaneously provide data as a constant stream. This is enough to overwhelm any person, in life as much as one who is near death. In O'Rowe's world, however, B experiences inter-dimensional travel in addition to her flying from city centre to the sea and back inland even after death. While she accepts her fate, B receives another chance when she returns to the world, reborn as the child of A's former student. In a sense, her memory was erased to make room for a new experience where she could begin a new life. Even at birth, there is the sensation of connection to the first person one encounters in this world. B describes the experience in positive terms: '[S]he's smiling down at me like you would at a child, her expression melancholy yet beguiled, and, though I don't know her at all, she evokes in me such love,' unaware that this was her mother in her past life (45). As a newborn, B is immediately thrust into an unknown experience. The one sensation she feels a deep desire to fulfil is for love and connection to this person. What appeared to be the full encapsulation of globalization, via loss of selfhood, is replaced with a new sense of belonging and companionship.

In the same way, this connection is reciprocated and expanded through A. The experience leaves such a mark on both the newborn B and A that the mother can think of nothing else but the need to reconcile all past grievances with her daughter. A narrates: 'And somehow, after this ill-fated night, my failed crusade, misguided right from the start, this child does something to my heart, recalls to me my own child's birth, the sense I had of being earthed to the world as joy unfurled around me, bound me to her and, through her, made me whole' (39). Similar to B becoming filled with joy and purpose in her new life, A rejects the emptiness caused by a separation from her daughter. A experienced Dublin in almost unimaginable ways to save a life that was not even meant for her to save. The mother wants to make amends, and she unknowingly has through her generous spirit and connection with the baby girl. But A does not recognize this as the fulfilment of her goal. Her final moments in the play express the feeling that she has achieved what she set out to do, even if she had no awareness of what she was seeking.

The final moments of C's narrative take a slightly different turn from the other stories as he races through Dublin driving a truck only to then steal a Mercedes and hopefully avoid capture. His soul, however, finds and catches him only to return him to the very crane where B fell near the play's beginning. The demon impales C on his tail and throws him off the side of the crane, catching him after the fall and also disembowelling him as he hangs above Dublin city. A crowd gathers below and, instead of great fear and shame, C is overcome with the desire to sing. As death comes to him, the shy man is able to perform. He receives approval and applause for his rendition of Bette Midler's 'Wind Beneath My Wings.' While this event goes beyond even fantastical into an almost absurd narrative trick, C's desire for social acceptance remains tethered to his existence. No longer is he the object of scorn nor does he harbour thoughts of hatred toward his fellow man now that they have inspired his change of heart. The moment of change may seem at odds with the world created by the rotating monologues, but in fact this has produced a picture of globalization that magnifies each aspect. This moment came because of his need to fit into society which had slowly neglected him due to its overwhelming expansiveness. But it is only through his final moment of achievement (in the eyes and ears of society) that he is able to transcend the need to escape. Instead, C embraces these connections and banishes the formerly negative views that globalization had heaped upon him.

C's evolution inspires a change of heart in his soul as it also complicates the audience's opinions on his experience. The idea of globalization as a consumptive, culture-driven definition neglects the complexity of human life. Even as the world seems to shrink, further isolating individuals, O'Rowe's tale shows that even diverse and divisive lives parallel and collide as part of the workings of daily life. Granted, one would hardly describe these stories as normal, but one must recall the monologues began as unassuming experiences of monotony and loneliness. Once each narrator moved beyond the basic fears of life in the contemporary world, the necessity of mobility and connection to others becomes integral to his or her understanding of the world. A sought solace in the need to help others, even though it was mediated by voices on the other end of a phone line. B sequestered herself to a life of routine, television, and microwave dinners. C, worst of all, actively fought connections, preferring to show his dissatisfaction with the globalized world and its adulation of celebrities and extroverts through violence against other loners in the same position as himself. But O'Rowe does not allow these characters to wallow in their own self-pity. Rather his play presents a world that is deeply consumed by its need for interconnectivity, but that does not necessarily negate the necessity for an individual relating to another person. Lonergan argues that 'Monologue may be popular because the intimacy between actors and audience reasserts community when, thanks to globalization, audiences are experiencing excessive level of individualization' (185). Characters and viewers share this intimacy. *Terminus* highlights the vast array of people with whom a singular entity might interact on any given day. This recognition comes among the depression and feelings of isolation, but once the characters extend their prospects for interconnection they finally admit to the necessity for human relationships. The monologue (and by association, *Terminus*) presents inclusivity in a world that seems to celebrate exclusivity and separation. Even when characters stand separated on a mostly bare stage, they still stand together in a room with an audience.

In summation, O'Rowe's exploration of solitude, character mobility, and questioning of traditional moral boundaries leads to a vision of hopeful globalized societies. While many critics would still emphasize the playwright's use of gratuitous violence, the reality of the contemporary world can be seen as equally brutal given the ubiquity of technology and media sources reinforcing isolation while alleging connectivity. This fact situates the three tales within a heightened reality. Audiences listen to the characters sharing their thoughts and emotions, which drive every human, but each entity returns to the need for human interaction in a world that would otherwise ignore the individual in favour of the shrinking global experience. O'Rowe's play portrays the contemporary experience as one of filling up rather than deflating. People can transcend stereotypes and expectations. Characters choose to connect rather than accepting solitude. In the end, even the worst person can reconcile their difficult past. As C says in the play's final line: 'I've heard tell that even the Devil remembered Heaven after he fell' (50).

Works Cited

Collins-Hughes, Laura. 'Grisly Scenes, In the Mind's Eye.' *The Boston Globe* 4 Feb. 2011.

Dawkins, Richard. *The Extended Phenotype: The Long Reach of the Gene*. Oxford: Oxford University Press, 1999.

Derrida, Jacques. *Negotiations: Interventions and Interviews 1971-2001*. Ed. and Trans. E. Rottenberg. Stanford, CA: Stanford University Press, 2002.

Grene, Nicholas. *The Politics of Irish Drama*. Cambridge: Cambridge University Press, 1999.

Keating, Sara. 'Is Martin McDonagh an Irish Playwright?' *The Theatre of Martin McDonagh: A World of Savage Stories*. Ed. Lilian Chambers and Eamonn Jordan. Dublin: Carysfort Press, 2006: 281-294.

Logan, Brian. '*Terminus* – Review.' *The Guardian* (UK), 5 Apr. 2011.

Lonergan, Patrick. *Theatre and Globalization: Irish Drama in the Celtic Tiger Era*. Basingstoke: Palgrave Macmillan, 2009.

Murphy, Tom. 'Introduction.' *Tom Murphy Plays: One*. London: Methuen, 1992.

O'Rowe, Mark. *Terminus*. London: Nick Hern, 2007.

Raab, Michael. 'Mark O'Rowe.' *The Methuen Drama Guide to Contemporary Irish Playwrights*. Ed. Martin Middeke and Peter Paul Schnierer. London: Methuen, 2010: 345-364.

Robertson, Roland. *Globalization: Social Theory and Global Culture*. London: Sage, 1992.

Singleton, Brian. '*Terminus* by Mark O'Rowe.' *Irish Theatre Magazine*. 4 July 2007.

Syke, Lloyd Bradford. 'Review: *Terminus*.' *Crikey*. Private Media Pty Ltd., 14 June 2011.

Wright, Robert. *The Moral Animal: Why We Are the Way We Are*. New York: Vintage Books, 1995.

Zinoman, Jason. 'For Him, the Devil Is in the Rhymes.' *New York Times*, 13 Jan. 2008.

10 | Violated Sanctuaries:
The Screenplays of Mark O'Rowe

Harvey O'Brien

Although Mark O'Rowe is best known as a playwright, he is also a screenwriter and fledgling screen director. This chapter focuses on the film work, raising the question of how a writer retains authorial presence in a process as transformative as filmmaking. To date O'Rowe has only actually directed one short: *debris* (2013), and, in spite of a BAFTA nomination for Breakthrough Talent for *Boy A* (2007) and an IFTA win for Best Script for *Intermission* (2003), the playwright's voice isn't as clearly heard on film as it is on the stage. Indeed, despite writing four successful feature-length films, his name appears surprisingly infrequently in recent writing on Irish film. Even in Dióg O'Connell's *New Irish Storytellers: Narrative Strategies in Film* (Intellect, 2011), he features only in a footnote.[12] It probably doesn't help that *Boy A* and *Broken* (2012) are adaptations (of the novels by Jonathan Trigell and Daniel Clay respectively), and that screenwriters are often under-recognized as the co-creators of the finished film. There are nonetheless authorial continuities across the screen-writings of Mark O'Rowe that merit some elaboration, and this essay will outline them by breaking the filmography into three sections: original feature screenplays; adaptations; and shorts.

Screenplay

In a business where teams of accredited writers beat an original screenplay into the final shooting script, it is a wonder that any discernible shreds of authorial voice endure in the finished product at

---

[12] O'Connell, 2011: 64n.

all. A screenplay is a rather unique object. It doesn't really have a life of its own, not the way a novel or a playscript does, and certainly not the way a film does. Writing a screenplay is a creative act that requires skill to produce a finished crafted object, but the finished screenplay is both something definite and nothing at all. As Mark O'Thomas remarks, whereas a playscript can be published and read with a view to repeated performance and revision, a published screenplay is 'a frozen entity' (237) which, when published, is more a souvenir than a literary/textual object. Except in the very few cases of remakes that purport to replicate faithfully the original, most published screenplays are 'locked' literary records of a completed audio-visual media object in which the screenplay is literally not visible.

Kathryn Millard likens the screenplay to a 'prototype' (142), O'Thomas calls it a 'blueprint' (237), and Jill Nelmes explains that the screenplay is 'considered merely the first stage towards the final product, the feature film, and therefore not on a creative par with the stage play, prose, or poetry, which are more immediate creative forms with a less complex production process' (1). Indeed, Nelmes's edited volume *Analysing the Screenplay* is one of the very few academic studies of the form.

Sometimes analysing a screenwriter's contribution to a feature film isn't therefore so much about the nuance of the realized moment on screen as experienced by the viewer in the final 'filmed' version, as it is about the architecture of plot and character and the recurring dramatic and thematic motifs that tie them together. It is also at least partly about the dialogue, although this too is often subject to significant revision, even in performance. The words of the screenwriter are most often less sacrosanct than those of the playwright, although this depends on the conditions of production, particularly the proclivities of the personnel for cinematic authorship.

If one of the primary rules of academic film analysis is to avoid a reliance on plot and character, the reverse is arguably true in the analysis of screenwriting. That said, there is a definite argument in favour of examining the role of character relative to plot. There are two configurations. On one hand, there are screenplays where the characters seem comparatively autonomous, exceeding the demands of the plot in exhibiting manners and behaviours that do not 'drive' the narrative. On the other, are the more well-behaved classical characters who function as the plot demands and are 'driven' by the narrative. Steven Price describes this in terms of 'contained' and 'open' texts. Price compares the structuralist model of a classic, rigid Aristotlean text as taught by Hollywood screenwriting manuals via Syd Field or Robert McKee with a looser form of screenplay in flux that incorporates on-site characterization in performance such as, in his example, Orson Welles clearly 'authoring' Harry Lime in *The Third Man* (1949) in ways that exceed the original conception of the character.

In the films written by Mark O'Rowe we can see continuities in the construction of plot and character and their arrangement relative to one another, and also, to a more limited degree, in dialogue that brings elements of both the 'contained' and 'open' approaches into play and reflect a distinctive authorial voice. O'Rowe's characters seem to actively struggle to 'open' the text in order to escape the containment of plot. They seem to seek that elusive sanctuary of self-creation and self-realization. They idiomatically grapple with a type of self-expression that allows them to assert their awareness and their significance in the cosmos: oscillating between brutish physicality and delimited but articulate intellectual observation of their own actions, as if trying to come to grips with them amid the panic of the reaction-response that allows them to survive at all. The characters are usually incapable of genuine reflectiveness as a result, and never quite understand their own actions in context. Rather than being active protagonists in the mould of classical heroes, they end up being driven by events and circumstances, and inevitably the sanctuary they create is violated as necessity reasserts its drive towards resolution and death. Of course, as Death himself assures us at the end of *Perrier's Bounty* – voiced by Gabriel Byrne, the 'obscure and enigmatic' narrator of the film – his existence alone is proof 'that each of us is significant in this vast and degenerate cosmos.' This off-screen commentating voice suggests the characters are not alone in this authored universe, and neither are we, who are being addressed, after all.

The Original Screenplays: *Intermission* (2003) and *Perrier's Bounty* (2009)

Intermission was the first of O'Rowe's collaborations with director John Crowley, who would also direct *Boy A*. The film was released at the height of the Celtic Tiger period in Irish cinema, during which Irish cinema on the whole exhibited a brash satisfaction with the modernization of Irish urban culture through recourse to socio-politically affirmational genre models, primarily comedy and gangster films, which ultimately uphold the status quo.

Buoyed by an influx of international investment in the Irish film industry, comedies like *About Adam* (2000), *When Brendan Met Trudy*

(2000), and *Goldfish Memory* (2003) posited a modern and hedonistic Ireland in which the identity politics of past generations were increasingly irrelevant. Meanwhile, crime films like *Accelerator* (2000), *Headrush* (2003), and *Man About Dog* (2004) cheerfully delved into the margins with much the same ethos of open-market pleasure-seeking: presenting Ireland as a landscape full of possibilities for making and spending money on an inflated lifestyle.

Intermission combines and parodies both of these generic frames through a structure that alternates between the two. The romantic comedy involves the separation of John (Cillian Murphy) and Deirdre (Kelly Macdonald), the classic boy-girl combination whose paused relationship is tested by the events that transpire in the film. Among those events are the pursuit of hardened thief Lehiff (Colin Farrell) by a dogged cop, Gerry Lynch (Colm Meaney), with this second 'couple' comprising the classic duology of the standard gangster film. The generic frames are brought into direct contact with one another by having John drawn into Lehiff's plan to kidnap middle-aged banker Sam (Michael McElhatton), who is currently having an extramarital affair with Deirdre.

Perrier's Bounty largely eschews male-female romance. Michael, a small-time loser who owes money to titular crime boss Darren Perrier (Brendan Gleeson), evinces a certain level of care and concern for his suicidal neighbour Brenda (Jodie Whitaker), who accompanies him on his evasive manoeuvres through Dublin, and seems eager to convince her that her boyfriend Shamie (Padraic Delaney) is not good enough for her. But Michael's own family trauma, where he believes he is responsible for a violent attack on his mother, seems to keep him from hope for a romance of his own. His disconnection is brought into relief by his dying father's (Jim Broadbent) attempts at reconciliation, driving towards family unity and catharsis before his death. In this way the film deploys the romantic comedy's essential and integral movement towards integration and coupling through the trope of family that continues to dominate Irish film. Family is the ultimate sanctuary, albeit one that remains deliberately obscure even at the film's finale where Michael's mother is glimpsed as an out-of-focus figure standing in the sea.

The film does present one emotionally-committed romantic couple – the gangsters Ivan (Michael McElhatton) and Orlando (Don Wycherley) – but this too is shattered. Their romance is not revealed until after Orlando's death (his is the body buried on the hillside by Jim and Michael), and partly triggers the titular bounty that Perrier puts on

Michael's head; again the generic strands intersect on a structural level that takes an obtuse angle on formula.

In both films, O'Rowe presents blocks of narrative in which the characters actively engage with and work against the generic frame. Though the broad contours of their behaviour are within expected norms, and O'Rowe obeys the rules and delivers the pleasures of a genre entertainment, there is a constant sense that these individuals would rather not be behaving as they do, as if they are aware there is another state of existence they just might be able to escape to. This is a visible aspect of characterization even when characters broadly adhere to generic type, and this allows O'Rowe to throw in some surprises.

The most famous surprise is probably at the opening of *Intermission* where Lehiff, at this point his role unknown to the audience, speaks playfully and seductively to a young waitress (Kerry Condon) in a café. It might be the start of a romantic comedy, but the harmonic oasis of male-female banter is violently disrupted when Lehiff warns her that he might be any sort of scumbag, and proves it by punching her in the face before robbing the register and making a break for it with the cash. The collision between generic frames and the refusal to constrain characterization couldn't be more clearly underlined, except that it is, because O'Rowe gives Lehiff the line of dialogue 'You never know what's going to happen.'

Both *Intermission* and *Perrier's Bounty* also demonstrate a preoccupation with the idea of the warrior. In a world in which your capacity to survive is measured by the degree to which, how, and why you wield violence, his characters are frequently envisioned as 'warrior souls' as Lynch puts it in *Intermission*. This is a carry-over from O'Rowe's plays, of course, as noted by Eamonn Jordan, who examines the deployment of the image of Bruce Lee in *Howie the Rookie* (1999). Jordan notes that O'Rowe's warriors are 'without a classical class grievance' (122) in spite of their situation within the twentieth-century urban underclass. O'Rowe's characters struggle with economic constraint and the constant sense of lack and under-privilege, but their primary spiritual motivation seems to be a need for a moment's rest from the pressure of inevitable fate, rather than upward mobility or class solidarity.

O'Rowe's protagonists are characters without master-plans. They are warriors, not generals. Even in the world of the gangster film, with its capos and lieutenants, O'Rowe makes unusual choices in how the narrative frames and engages these characters. In *Perrier's Bounty*, even Perrier seems oddly disconnected from his empire, and the respect he receives from the symbolically named Mutt (Liam Cunningham) does not ultimately save the latter from Perrier's casual disregard for their temporary alliance. Perrier shoots him down like the proverbial dog, something he has already done in the film with actual dogs, an act which comes back to haunt him at the finale.

Michael is shown as a natural fighter, and one with a righteous and protective side. He tries to protect Brenda from her cheating boyfriend and he tried to protect his family from local thugs. That his actions frequently trigger destructive reprisal is not seen as his fault, which is not to say that his aggression isn't extreme or his capacity to carry out violent acts is wholly restricted. Michael, like Jim, is a just warrior, reactive and protective, and ultimately blameless, like the ill-fated 'warrior dogs' Achilles and Apollo, dismissively shot down by Perrier and later buried on the same hilltop as Orlando. Likewise John in *Intermission* (both characters played by the same actor, note) gets drawn into criminality and violence that he really isn't part of, which isn't to say he isn't capable of doing what needs to be done.

Ultimately, it is not so much a matter of class grievance, as Jordan says, but of a much deeper engagement with the primal forces of fate (and narrative structure). This theme is addressed in a pronounced way in *Intermission*, where Lynch is being courted by ambitious journalist Ben (Tomás Ó Súilleabháin) to make a reality TV show about the challenges faced by the modern Irish cop on the mean streets of Celtic Tiger Dublin. Though Lynch likes to listen to Clannad on his car stereo, an affectation which throws the characterization into relief, he is a pugilistic, domineering would-be Alpha male who also behaves like a dog by urinating on Lehiff in a pub toilet to show him who's boss, and who relishes the idea of having his ego stroked by a TV show. He suggests calling it 'Hard as Nails Cunts'. O'Rowe satirizes contemporary reality television's preoccupation with truth and the real (both of which are always absent) by presenting Lynch as another of O'Rowe's fantasists – making up his own world in which he is master of his own destiny, and finding he is not.

There is some irony in his statement at the end of the film that Ben is, like himself, a 'warrior soul', as the bedraggled, bandaged, and injured Lynch delivers this line while Ben is watching and re-watching the tape of the shooting of Lehiff. Though Lynch has received the hero's credit for bringing down the notorious criminal, it is revealed that Ben has in fact pulled the trigger after picking up Lynch's gun in a confrontation on a rural hillside where the classical cop and robber showdown has not gone according to plan. Like in *Perrier's Bounty*, the violence is misdirected and accidental, but not without consequence. The overall structure O'Rowe presents therefore determines that the film must operate in the realm of parody, satire, and irony. It must be reflexive to a degree, self-aware in large measure, and must ultimately oscillate between an open and contained narrative in which his characters, like those on stage, articulate their sense of self and being against a struggle to navigate and negotiate their lived reality. They are dogs of war in search of sanctuary, but are not quite sure what that even is.

The Adaptations: *Boy A* (2007) and *Broken* (2012)

Boy A and *Broken* both problematize attributions of authorship and intentionality, given they are adapted from works by other creative artists. Though *Boy A* was directed by John Crowley, whose working relationship with O'Rowe through *Intermission* suggests a degree of creative symbiosis, *Broken* was directed by theatre director Rufus Norris, making his feature debut. These are two very different films, both from each other and from the original features written by O'Rowe. Both films are more experimental in structure, taking the broadly playful generic revisionism of *Intermission* and *Perrier's Bounty* deeper into drama. Both films nonetheless also deal explicitly with the theme of violated sanctuaries, and feature characters that lack the means to articulate their dilemmas, making them simpatico with O'Rowe's sensibility. The pronounced warrior element falls largely away, but there is a strong dimension of a struggle for survival in both films.

In *Boy A*, Jack (Andrew Garfield) is a juvenile offender who participated in a murder as a child but is now rehabilitated. He is released from prison as an adult under supervision by Terry (Peter Mullan), an enthusiastic mentor, whose relationship with his own son is less ideal. In order to protect himself, Jack cannot reveal his past to anyone and though he revels in the small joys of his new freedom – a pair of new sneakers, some recreational narcotics on a night out with friends – he is haunted by nightmares. These dreams reveal the details of his crime in flashback, shaping both how we sees his present and future possibilities. The sneakers, for example, trigger a motivated flashback to a pair of sneakers on feet dangling unnaturally in mid-air, revealed, eventually, to be worn by the boy who goaded Jack into the murder, and who was subsequently lynched by other inmates in prison.

At first Jack seems to successfully build a new life. He takes a job, makes some friends, and pursues a passionate relationship with co-worker Michelle (Katie Lyons), but his emotional needs are very deep, and his sense of vulnerability that comes from the violence he himself has perpetrated makes his very ordinary life a visibly great struggle. When he bravely rescues a child from the aftermath of a motor vehicle accident, the media spotlight turns on him and his past is uncovered (partly through the intervention of Terry's jealous son), shattering the sanctuary he had so briefly inhabited. At the end of the film Jack stands on Blackpool pier, hanging over the edge and holding on to the railing, contemplating the dark water below, his head filled with imagined conversations and fantasies of how things might have gone. The film ends without explicit resolution, but its narrative and thematic trajectory is clearly not redemptive.

O'Rowe brings us inside the mind of a protagonist to explore conflicts between the inner and outer worlds, another of the novelistic techniques identified by Steven Price as being outside the demesne of ordinary screenwriting. Direct access to the thoughts and inner life of characters, Price tells us, is usually embodied in formal terms through montage or voiceover, both suspect modes of cinematic narration: 'the montage, besides now being rather clichéd, cannot capture individual voice the way that prose narration can. Meanwhile, voiceover has often been dismissed in film criticism as a manipulative literary device that falls victim to the 'specificity thesis" (204); the way in which a screenplay is a unique object with no status beyond the finished feature film.

The challenge for O'Rowe in both *Boy A* and *Broken* is the prose basis of the works he is adapting, and he overcomes it by dealing explicitly with the dynamics of internal versus external narration in the structure. The gap between the two can be understood relative to the notion of open and contained texts examined earlier, and which, as we have seen, is a recurring structuring convention in O'Rowe's work. As *Intermission* and *Perrier's Bounty* move between generic registers while their characters struggle against them, so *Boy A* and *Broken* defy cine-narrational constraint by contrasting a dynamic inner life with a static outer one. The characters are *shown* to have an inner and outer world through a narrative structure that oscillates between them, shifting from public to private spaces in ways that reveal the connectedness of these separate worlds.

The delicate way Jack physically navigates his world in *Boy A* suggests his inner experience, as does the focus on the small details in which he revels. Like O'Rowe's stage monologues or the struggle for articulation and eloquence in his original features, Jack's entire experience is a mode of dialectical self-narration relative to an external world that could collapse at any time. That we end up inside his head with an explicit voiceover at the finale is no surprise, because that is where we have always been.

Broken is even more explicit about its use of an internal world imperfectly reflected by the external one we see. The plot of the novel and the film consciously recycle Harper Lee's *To Kill a Mockingbird*, and presents the ultimate violation of sanctuary in the shattering of the membrane of childhood perception. A young girl named Skunk (Eloise Laurence) sees an act of previously inconceivable violence that forces her to search for meaning and order in the adult world, hitherto understandable through the mediation of her reliable lawyer father Archie (Tim Roth). Though the film does not give its protagonist access to a mode of literary direct address like a voiceover, it again deploys structure to suggest a break in cinematic contiguity.

In basic narrative terms, it presents its defining moment quickly when Skunk sees neighbour and lone parent Bob Oswald (Rory Kinnear) savagely beat slow-witted but seemingly harmless local lad Rick Buckley (Robert Emms), an act he later repeats on Skunk's teacher Mike Kiernan (Cillian Murphy). Oswald is, ironically, concerned with his own three daughters' innocence, which the film shows us is beyond saving. Skunk therefore confronts a world of sexuality and violence without quite understanding it. In dramatic and thematic terms, as noted, the shadow of Harper Lee hangs heavily over the proceedings, and from the point of view of O'Rowe's contribution, he is here juggling the influences of three other creative artists, including director Norris, novelist Clay, and Lee.

O'Rowe finds in this jumble some correlation with his own previous work, not least in the way in which the entire experience is revealed to be a psychic negotiation taking place inside Skunk's mind as she lies in a coma. She has slipped into a diabetic coma following a series of events that bring her to Rick's house on the same night that Oswald's middle child dies from complications resulting from pregnancy. In this revision of Lee's original plot, Oswald becomes Boo Radley, and saves Skunk by finding her in the Buckley household. She ends up recuperating in hospital, Archie by her side, contemplating the life she has lived and speculating as to its future. Like Jack in *Boy A*, Skunk is therefore in a place of temporary respite vulnerable to the threat of the external world and of death itself.

The film presents the potentialities of external life as a choice. Skunk might remain in her mind and never emerge. It refuses narrative clarity and shifts back and forward in time in ways we will see echoed in

O'Rowe's shorts, so there is an element of structural experimentation here that can be linked with the screenwriter's recurring concerns. Significantly, the place in Skunk's mind that signifies the choice to remain in death is a Church (a literal sanctuary) where all of her friends and family are gathered. She is also haunted by fragments of foresight – a vision of herself as an adult – and she eventually chooses life, reawakening into a world with which we must presume she has come to terms. Her dialogue with death has ended in temporary refusal, a reversal of the end of *Boy A*, and one noted with some scepticism by some reviewers, though it also echoes the positive ending of *To Kill a Mockingbird*.

The Shorts: *Epithet* (2012) and *debris* (2013)

Short films are a world unto themselves in film analysis, and can be seen as a legitimate and distinct form of cinema, like the short story or the sonnet in literature. Realistically though, shorts often serve in industrial terms as a kind of proving ground or experimental workshop for filmmakers looking on to bigger things. In the case of Mark O'Rowe's *debris*, this is likely true, though he has at the time of writing not made a feature directorial debut. However, *debris* and *Epithet* are fascinating texts in themselves, and worth some consideration.

Epithet is a serio-comic drama revolving around John (Patrick Stewart), an aging poet with a wandering eye, who has used the ultimate appellation of insult in referring to his soon to be ex-wife. As he expounds smugly and wearily to his friend Richard (Matthew Marsh) about the ease with which women fall upon him, the film flashes backward and forward to a seduction-in-progress over the dinner table. As John explains to Richard that he finds it hard to keep up the pretence that life has meaning, he tells young Rebecca (Aimee Ffion Edwards) of an incident of violence he witnessed that same day. Following their initial conversation, John and Richard see a young woman sitting stricken under a tree in the park, holding in her bloodied guts. This is an incident without motivation, context, or explanation, and there is no narrative follow-through other than John recounting the tale to Rebecca. In the logic of John's world, the event has no real meaning and he has been unmoved, but as he presents the story and his role in it to Rebecca over dinner, it becomes a profound, moving moment of an encounter with violence which, he explains, is 'beyond analysis, beyond intellect'. His seduction appears to have worked and Rebecca is about to agree to spend the night with him when he is suddenly grabbed from behind by his soon to be ex-brother-in-law,

Alan (Richard McCabe) screaming 'Did you call my sister a cunt, you pretentious fucking faggot?' as he repeatedly punches him in the face, eventually concluding 'You're the cunt.' Epithet indeed.

The peculiar genesis of *Epithet* lies in theatre director Angus Jackson's production of Edward Bond's *Bingo* at the Young Vic in 2012. It features members of the cast of that production and was directed by Jackson from a script by O'Rowe, and shot in two days around Paris Gardens on the Southwark in London. According to Jackson,[13] the brief from the Young Vic, who sponsored the production, was that it be inspired by the play (which deals with Shakespeare's latter years as a world-weary poet) and be bold in approach. He asked O'Rowe to come up with something contemporary, and this was the result.

The shocking conclusion recalls the similar tonal shift at the opening of *Intermission*, although in this case it is not a preface but a (literal) punch-line. Self-aggrandizing pedantry is interrupted by an act of extreme violence, which, while sudden, is not without some preface. Its concern with fantasies of male control and sexual domination shattered by violence is also familiar terrain for O'Rowe, as is the fascination with time, now emerging as a definite element of how he navigates cinematic modes of narration.

The film begins with John and Rebecca having dinner, then cuts to John and Richard in conversation. In 'real time' terms this is a move from future to past, or present to past, but the viewer is not quite certain of this until the explosive conclusion definitely locates the moment of violence as an indisputable, eruptive present. By tracking back and forth between timeframes, the script critiques its characters through the narrative structure by stripping the timeline of cause and effect. The crosscutting forces the viewer to consider if John's attitude towards women and performance is ultimately 'deserving' of his fate. The 'cause' of the beating itself is not directly seen or heard, but the consequence of it runs throughout the entire timeline of the film, framing our understanding of John, whom we see in two dimensions: as smug lothario and active seducer. Even so, we do not see him use the epithet or act overtly aggressively towards his wife. As such, we identify with his confident intelligence and wry sense of humour at first; then perhaps begin to wonder at his coldness as he uses the death of the girl to get another into bed, which culminates so suddenly in the classic 'punishment' resolution. This satisfies our sense of emotional justice while also shocking the viewer.

---

[13] See Jackson, 2012.

The violence is doubly shocking because it also shatters the otherwise intellectual, verbal, frame of the drama. The alternation between the indoor and outdoor locations also visually changes the tone, but again this is an effect of direction (though it is suggested in the dialogue too, given the two 'faces' of John we see in each respective locale). In both cases, however, there is very little 'action': the characters are seated on a bench, at a dinner table, or talking as they stroll through the London streets. There is no real physical action other than the encounter with the girl, which is itself passive both in narrative terms, as noted, and as 'action', because we do not see the stabbing or the response – just the girl sitting, panting, and holding her stomach with bloodied hands. It is a moment of pure spectacle, but not of action.

The beating, by contrast, is all action. It is a moment of absolute physicality, kinaesthetically impactful and intentionally disruptive of the verbal frame. The quiet seduction is completely shattered by a physical expression we have been unintentionally pre-informed by John will be 'beyond intellect'. The intellectual sanctuary is viscerally violated. The punching is rapid, relentless, and peppered by verbal aggression, and John, the man whose 'action' to date has been all intellect from the perspective of what the viewer has seen, is the passive recipient of punishment. The film began with him dismissing Alan's physical capacities as 'an overweight accountant', but ends with a series of counterpoints, including proof that in fact John is not able to 'take' him, but ends up 'taking' what Alan dishes out. This dynamic evokes remarks by Cathy Leeney with regard to O'Rowe's dramaturgy where passivity, in her view, is the (gendered) response to violence where 'Power is defined as violence and language is the only field available for resistance or denial' (115). She is writing here about *Crestfall*, but the point is taken, and is complicated here by the parodic evocation of John's use of language as a kind of violence or at least domination, which certainly does not give him either power or resistance.

The deployment of fragmented time is continued in *debris*, as is the structural obfuscation of cause and effect. In story terms, David (Declan Conlon), a man on the brink of marriage with his current girlfriend Aisling (Joanne Campbell), has a chance encounter with Margaret (Aisling O'Sullivan), the sister of his former and now deceased girlfriend, Catherine (Catherine Walker). Their conversation forces him to ask complex questions about his complicity in Catherine's death. Catherine killed herself years before, following an argument with David. Margaret clearly believes David to have been responsible for tipping Catherine over the edge by what he said to her (particularly the film's opening line 'Now, fuck off!'), but, as the flashbacks reveal, the dynamics of their last conversation as David recalls them were different from what Catherine told her sister.

The compressed temporality of the short film again allows O'Rowe a greater degree of motivated juxtaposition. *debris* ambitiously attempts to juggle three timelines to explore the threads of interpersonal conflict and emotional consequence that have brought David to where he finds himself as the film ends – sobbing in Aisling's arms. The film begins with the audience being thrown into the middle of a heated row between David and Catherine, a moment that has no past, and no future until we realize that the opening of the film is part of a lingering past that haunts him, like the motivated flashbacks in *Boy A*. The meeting with Margaret triggers that haunting, suggesting perhaps that the opening flashback is itself a psychic flash-forward rather than a document of the past as a present moment, and all of this is ultimately presented as the psychic ruminations of the protagonist, who ends the film as noted, crying in the arms of his new fiancé for reasons we now understand. David becomes something like Jack in *Boy A*, possessed of a deep inner life visible only through an imperfect external representation revealed by the structure of the screenplay to have greater dimensionality.

As a director, O'Rowe reveals a predilection for shots with long duration. However the crosscutting between timeframes abandons causality on the level of narrative. Unlike in *Epithet*, the audience is not given a clear visual distinction between the variant timeframes. In the former film, warm lighting and a shift between medium and close-up shots distinguish intimate and performative moments. The palette of *debris* is essentially uniform blue-grey, making for no clear visual distinction between space, place, and time. This makes it a more confusing film than *Epithet*, relying less on a humourous disruption of temporal contiguity, instead building its world out of broken shards of contiguous space and time.

The film is also reminiscent of *Broken* in the way the plot unfolds. As *Broken* transpired to be the fevered dreams of a girl in a coma so *debris* is a presentation of the shattered psyche, sifting through the causes and effects of its trauma, searching amid the debris for the shards of catharsis. Like in *Epithet*, the motivating incident isn't really visualized. Yes, we hear David tell Catherine to fuck off, but we do not see her death or any scenes of his immediate response to that significant moment of decisive action. We do see and hear more of the crucial conversation between them, though. In fact, the last moments of what we now understand to be the past are of David saying he doesn't want this to end, which suggests a vacillation that became a resolution only because of an action the audience does not see. Again, narrative causality is consciously frustrated by omission, though emotional consequence weighs heavily. David cries; an outpouring of inchoate expression most likely not understood by Aisling, who cradles him.

The theme of sanctuary is also paramount here, because to Aisling, David is a man in whose 'manly arms' she feels 'protected' and 'secure'. Like all of O'Rowe's states of bliss, this is shown to be more vulnerable than it would appear. David's collapse is a consequence of his memories forcefully coming to the surface upon meeting Margaret, a trigger which brings his past into conflict with his present and forces him to confront the consequence of the one for the other. His strength, perhaps built over time through disavowal, denial, or just the distance of time, is insufficient to prevent the violation of his temporary sanctuary and now, perhaps, causes Aisling too to consider whether she is secure after all. Why, after all, is David crying?

Conclusion

Mark O'Rowe's film scripts demonstrate a consistent refraction of structuring conventions that turn narratives back upon themselves and problematize the ways in which we understand the relationship between plot and character. Like his plays, his film-writing presents partially articulate individuals struggling to make sense of a chaotic and violent world that they navigate partly on instinct. Across features, adaptations, and shorts, his voice stands outside and apart from the world of the film, almost like a commentator rather than a narrator. It is remarkable that this level of authorial coherence endures through the work of directors who have varying degrees of their own authorial distinction, particularly given the real-world process by which screenplays become motion pictures.

Works Cited

Jackson, Angus. 'Shakespeare, bear-baiting and bad language: how we made *Epithet.*' *The Guardian* Thursday 19 April 2012. Available online http://www.theguardian.com

Jordan, Eamonn. 'Project Mayhem: Mark O'Rowe's 'Howie the Rookie.'' *The Irish Review* No. 35 Summer 2007, 117-131.

Leeney, Cathy. 'Men in No-Man's Land: Performing Urban Liminal Spaces in Two Plays by Mark O'Rowe.' *The Irish Review* No. 35 Summer 2007, 108-116.

Mamet, David. 'Memo to writers of The Unit' (provenance unclear – 'leaked' document). Web. http://filmmakeriq.com/2011/02/david-mamets-screenwriting-rules/. Accessed 31 October, 2013.

Nelmes, Jill (ed.) *Analysing the Screenplay*. London and New York: Routledge, 2011.

Nelmes, Jill. 'Realism and Screenplay Dialogue'. Jill Nelmes (ed.) *Analysing the Screenplay*. New York and London: Routledge, 2011, 217-236.

Millard, Kathryn. 'The Screenplay as Prototype.' Jill Nelmes (ed.). *Analysing the Screenplay*. New York and London: Routledge, 2011, 142-157.

Price, Steven. 'Character in the Screenplay Text.' Jill Nelmes (ed.). *Analysing the Screenplay*. New York and London: Routledge, 2011, 201-216.

O'Connell, Dióg. *New Irish Storytellers: Narrative Strategies in Film*. Bristol. Intellect Press. 2011.

O'Thomas, Mark. 'Analysing the Screenplay: A Comparative Approach.' Jill Nelmes (ed.). *Analysing the Screenplay*. New York and London: Routledge, 2011, 237-250.

11 | Our Few and Evil Days

Emilie Pine

Mark O'Rowe's new play *Our Few and Evil Days* (Abbey Theatre, October 2014) is patterned by recurring themes of love and loss, hope and its unsettling impossibility, and the rising of a great darkness. The premise sounds unlikely, almost unbelievable; as one of the characters, Margaret, says it's 'crazy'. Three men are invited into a family home, two are thrown out, one remains. All of the men are looking for love, and they look to the women of the house to grant it to them. Their overtures begin with a request and end with violence. And one of the 'men' is a dead eleven-year-old boy, Jonathan.

Giving more than an elusive impression of the play involves plot spoilers. Dennis (Tom Vaughan-Lawlor) is going out with Adele (Charlie Murphy), who brings him home to meet her parents. Dennis, it transpires, is only involved with Adele as a way of getting to Margaret (Sinéad Cusack), her mother, who is the unsuspecting target of his real ardour. Dennis promises Margaret he can 'heal' the sadness she carries with her following the disappearance of her 11-year-old son, Jonathan, two decades earlier. When Margaret insists Dennis leave her house, he breaks off all contact with Adele. Meanwhile, Adele leaves to support her friend-in-crisis, Belinda (who never appears onstage). When Belinda later takes her own life, after a series of betrayals by her boyfriend Gary, Gary (Ian-Lloyd Anderson) visits Adele at the family home to unsuccessfully petition for her forgiveness, claiming that his insecurity led him to test Belinda's love. Adele rejects this claim outright, showing Gary for the bully he really is. The greater bully, however, turns out to be her father, Michael (Ciarán Hinds), who beats Gary up before throwing him out of the house. Adele's shock at Michael acting 'like a savage' leads her to question her father's involvement in

Jonathan's disappearance. When she later expresses this fear to her mother, Margaret reassures her that Michael is innocent of any violence to Jonathan, and goes on to disclose the reason for Jonathan's disappearance: on that fateful night Margaret had woken from a drunken sleep to discover her son raping her. Through this confession, which muddies the positions of victim and perpetrator, the child is demonized and the father is released. Yet in a final scene between Margaret and Michael, it is revealed that following the rape Michael did kill Jonathan, and that the couple live out their time in this house waiting for Jonathan's ghost to appear and, horribly, re-enact his crime in a love/hate ordeal that Margaret suffers in order to see him again. We are left with a series of questions: What is real and not real? Who is the manipulator? Which is the evil time, the brutally honest nights or the superficially calm yet dishonest days? Though Margaret spends her nights in thrall to the apparition of her dead son, her message of hope for Michael is that 'we'll always have our days'. This comfort is dispelled, however, as the lights come down and the all too real figure of Jonathan appears, beseeching his mother, 'Why don't you love me Mammy?'

The recurrent tropes from O'Rowe's earlier work are easy to spot: men with mother issues, men who do violence (emotional or physical) to women in the name of love, women who put up with the violence in the name of love. Though these repeated manifestations of abuse are bizarre, the issues themselves are only too easily recognisable social realities. The final appearance of the ghostly Jonathan, however, firmly removes the play from the category of 'social comment', much as the demonic presence of character C in *Terminus* makes that play more of an exploration of human nature than a critique of the over-reached ambition of the Celtic Tiger boom. This is a tactic that O'Rowe excels at, mixing incongruity with tragedy, the ridiculous and the sublime, as in *Howie the Rookie* when the vicious killing of Howie is driven by a combination of the demise of a few tropical fish, an infested mattress, and the tragic death of his little brother.

In its fascination with the supernatural, *Our Few and Evil Days* also bears comparison with Conor McPherson's *Shining City*, which ends with a similar spectral appearance, as well as with McPherson's *The Weir*, where a woman grasps at the promise that her dead child is haunting her, as a way of re-enacting her role as mother. In that play, however, Valerie shares her story with a group of local men she meets when she moves to the country as a way of exorcising her ghosts. Yet in *Our Few and Evil Days*, Margaret and Michael remain in the house that the crime was committed in, and only share the full story with each other. This closed circle ensures that there can be no moving on or exorcism, and all three – mother, father and dead son – remain in a kind of eternal purgatory for which there is no healing. As with plays like *Crestfall* (2003) and *From Both Hips* (1997) O'Rowe uses *Our Few and Evil Days* as a vehicle for exploring the question 'What is the worst thing you can imagine happening?' The experiment here is whether he can cover the same territory in a nice middle class family home, and the answer is yes.

The play's realist framework, which matches O'Rowe's true-to-life dialogue with a painstakingly detailed set by Paul Wills, is key to this. The constant contrast of realism and the fantastical, catches the audience in an uneasy oscillation between normality and weirdness, morality and corruption. Moreover, the audience is implicated in this oscillatory action, as the mood shifts from the early comfortable laughter of recognition to the distinctly uncomfortable laughter of disbelief as later revelations make the family's history more clear. Even during the exposition of disturbing or delusional moments, the dialogue and delivery remain naturalistic and, in this context, the audience is provoked to wonder how to read the situation. Is this middle-class social comedy or something much darker? Audiences might expect the latter given O'Rowe's track record of plays which exploit and explore the criminal and merciless side of human nature through grotesque humour and confrontation; the combination of those characteristics, however, with the framework of a realistically-realized suburban family life in *Our Few and Evil Days*, is entirely unexpected.

Directing his own work on the Abbey's main stage, O'Rowe shifts the pace from fast and overlapping dialogue to slow and quiet moments of confession. The dialogue rings so true that it lends a precision to every moment. In previous plays, O'Rowe's use of monologue has been a powerful device embodying alienation and the breakdown of communication. Yet here, though the characters talk to each other, and exhort each other to speak, there is no sense of communion.

Much of the power of the play, and the audience's ability to invest in the characters despite their dreadful actions, is created by the towering performances of Sinéad Cusack as Margaret and Ciarán Hinds as Michael. Cusack's understated embodiment of Margaret, who is both invested in and distant from the life going on around her, and Hinds' gruff persona as a decent violent man, do much to anchor the play and give the twists and turns of the plot some gravitas. As their daughter, Charlie Murphy is suitably highly-strung, as the only character in the play who is honest, a quality that comes across as both a form of vulnerability and a defence mechanism. Tom Vaughan-Lawlor and Ian Lloyd-Anderson are convincing as Dennis and Gary, lovers-turned-strangers, although neither character is fully developed; their appearances onstage are relatively brief, mostly serving to set in train a new set of disclosures.

The set design by Paul Wills, in its heightened simulacra, is the perfect foil to the unlikely story played out within it, while Paul Keogan's lighting design precisely evokes a well-heeled family home, particularly in its evening glow. Only in the sound design, with music by Philip Stewart and Seán Mac Erlaine, is there a hint of the uncanny, as the scene transitions are accompanied by a scratching and rustling, something shifting unhappily behind the happy façade.

That something emerges at the end, in the conspiratorial pact between Margaret and Michael, and the unexpected appearance of Jonathan, who exposes the lie that homes are always safe spaces for children, and theatres safe spaces for audiences.

12 | A Tallaght of the Mind: In Conversation with Mark O'Rowe

Cormac O'Brien, UCD

Cormac O'Brien met with Mark O'Rowe on the afternoon of Friday, 6th September, 2013, in the upstairs bar of the Abbey Theatre.

COB: Can you tell me about the sequence of events that saw Mark O'Rowe, a regular guy from Tallaght, become Mark O'Rowe, the Award Winning Playwright?

MOR: I had a normal working-class upbringing, no artists or interest, really, in art in the family, but I liked to watch martial arts movies and I also had a love for horror literature; in fact, that's all I read for a while, but I suppose I finally got tired of that and graduated to more grown up stuff; the classics, Shakespeare, anything that I'd heard was worth reading, I'd read. Likewise, my viewing habits became more sophisticated. I look back now at interviews I did when I first started out writing, and when I talked about those early interests, I feel now I was being pushed a little to emphasize them, to talk about Kung-Fu movies, etcetera, because these were a convenient connection to the violence in my own work. Any artist's make-up comes from thousands of different sources, but people feel they need to put this straightforward narrative on it. Although I was probably a little bit complicit in that myself.

COB: I guess when we think about what we were watching on TV when you first broke through in the late 1990s, early 2000s – the likes of The Sopranos, Guy Richie movies, and Tarantino – well then, people were only too happy to make these easy links.

MOR: Yes. But then you get those comparisons which are really reductive. Earlier on I was kind of happy to say those connections were there, but later, looking back at the work, I thought, 'this isn't actually true,' or 'it's only a tiny part of the story.' Are these the only cultural touchstones people have if you put a gun in a story or an act of violence? Or is it that they want to reduce you to that, for other reasons?

COB: So, obviously you weren't just watching films back then, you were engaging critically? Were you watching these movies and wanting to write a screenplay?

MOR: No, no. Really, I never knew I wanted to write until I actually started to write, which was much later on. It's interesting that the genres I was interested in watching way back then were ones for which narrative, theme, characterization, any of the essential elements of drama, are secondary considerations. You watch them for their visceral qualities alone. So, no, there was really no critical engagement at all. Though, I suppose when you're reading someone like Stephen King, you don't realize that. Though you're coming at it for the horror fix or whatever, you're also getting a lot of other really valuable stuff, even if you're completely unaware of it; you're absorbing, and developing a taste, or a need, for the slightly better characterization or greater complexity and ideas he's giving you. And maybe that need increases over time, and so, to feed it, you move on to more ambitious writers.

COB: So it was very much an evolution.

MOR: Yes, but because I didn't go to college, it was self-led; a process of discovering for myself what I was interested in, because I didn't have a guide.

COB: Is that something you think has hampered you as a writer, not going to college?

MOR: No.

COB: Well, that leads me neatly into my next question. Do you think playwriting and screenwriting are taught skills or are they innate?

MOR: It's a tough one, isn't it? I mean, for me, writing is like heroin. I can't get through my day unless I've done some, so there's something in being a writer that is an addiction to the act, the process. When I started writing, I imitated writers I admired, and there's nothing wrong with that, copying your heroes. You develop your skills that way, and then, when you begin to find your own voice, you can let those heroes go.

COB: So, these writer heroes are almost like scaffolding?

MOR: I suppose. At the time, I was copying Mamet and Pinter, particularly Mamet; the rhythms, the repetitions, the stresses, the beats and pauses, his use of particular phrasing, the energy. I remember in the beginning trying out various scenes in a similar style to see if I could actually write dialogue, then looking back over it and thinking, 'yeah, that's not too bad.'

But then, I think dialogue is particularly difficult to learn. Everything else, structure, characterization, plotting, all that can be developed and improved on. But good dialogue, I think, is something you need to have a natural ear for. Though I may be wrong.

COB: What about other influences? You've mentioned the classics, but what classics specifically? You've mentioned Beckett and I can see that, particularly when I think of *Terminus* and Beckett's *Play*. And you did a 'stripped back' version of *Henry IV* relatively shortly after you did Made In China. So, there are all these hard hitters.

MOR: It was everyone, really; Tolstoy, Dostoyevsky, Dickens, Chekhov ... American crime literature figured hugely, actually, particularly the psychological darkness and dense plotting of James Ellroy, and the sheer musicality of language in Elmore Leonard's work. Then there was that almost biblical quality in William Faulkner or Cormac McCarthy, whose stuff is close to poetry for me. A lot of Americans and Russians there. Shakespeare, who I really only connected with quite late (though I had read him when I was younger), is a big influence nowadays. He's pretty much the pinnacle, really.

When I wrote *Howie the Rookie,* I was quite influenced by Brian Friel's *Faith Healer*, and by Conor McPherson's first three monologue plays, which I'd been given in a collection. I remember reading these and loving the idea of an actor just coming out and telling a story, and that each line brought a new thought or event or idea. I thought they were real page turners and brilliant pieces. So I decided to try a monologue myself and *Howie* was a real breakthrough for me, because the earlier plays were, to an extent, still imitations – or not exactly, but certainly me not going all the way, not allowing myself to give vent to what was deeper inside ...

COB: And I wonder was there a sense of you trying to write an 'Irish Play'? With your earliest works, *The Aspidistra Code* and *From Both Hips*, was there a sense that you were trying to fit into a tradition that you felt you had to fit into to be successful in Ireland?

MOR: Yes. Or maybe not quite that, but there was an element of looking at the type of new work that was being staged at the time and wondering why mine couldn't be more like that. *From Both Hips*, and *The Aspidistra Code* were, I suppose, crime comedies mixed with a bit of Pinter and a bit of kitchen-sink drama, but I was also trying to tone it down, I suppose, and keep it palatable, just like the plays I could see were being staged around me. And so they weren't personal enough in a way. *Howie the Rookie* was a breakthrough in the sense that it was purely me.

A couple of things influenced me *during* the writing of it. One was *The Wild Bunch*, the Sam Peckinpah movie. Beyond its undoubted brilliance as a piece of art, what got me was just the fact that it was so utterly uncompromising, and you could tell that Peckinpah didn't give a shit whether or not anyone else went for it. So, that was an influence, particularly in terms of my self-confidence. That 'fuck you' quality. I said I'm going to do that. I think, before then, there was also a fear of self-revelation; a fear that whatever parts of me the work might expose would be perceived as weaknesses, things to be ashamed of or whatever. Which, of course, is ridiculous. In fact, it's the exploration of these 'weaknesses' that often create the moments which move an audience the most.

Also, while I was writing *Howie* I was reading Beckett, specifically his novel *Molloy*. And mid-way through I discovered that, while the first half of the book was narrated by Molloy, all of a sudden, there was a shift mid-way through to another point of view; Moran's, the private detective who's hired to track him down. And I thought, 'Oh! Here's a different first-person point of view, a whole new narrative half-way into the story!' I loved that.

So, I thought, I'm going to do that in this play I'm working on (which, at the time, I thought would be a one-man show). I'm going to bring in a second narrator. Then I got to the end of *Molloy* and discovered that his narrators never meet and I thought, 'Wow. I don't even have to tie up my plot. I can just create a thematic or a metaphoric conclusion, like Beckett did.' Ultimately, in *Howie,* everything *did* tie together plot-wise, but knowing that it didn't *have to* gave me another boost of confidence. Also the fact that the novel's so odd and singular and, again, uncompromising. I wondered if Beckett ever had the thought 'will anyone go for this?' But, of course, the more of what's specifically you in a piece, the more people will connect with it. At least I think that's true. The deeper a place it comes from inside you, the deeper a place it goes to in an audience.

COB: So, it was very much a sense of you learning rules, in order to learn that there are no rules, so that you can then go on to make your own rules?

MOR: In retrospect, yes. But at the time, you're just thinking, 'oh I'll copy this,' or 'I'll try this,' or 'this might be a good idea,' and you're writing completely intuitively, really. I mean, you're using your intellect in terms of constructing your story, and making one thing lead to another, making it all make sense, but, really, your best work is done when your conscious, critical mind is turned off and you're writing blind, discovering it all as you go. So, yes, that sort of rule-breaking you mentioned, it's not something you do consciously.

COB: Your work is highly theatrical, or, to use an academic term, performative. You're not the solitary writer in fingerless gloves, working alone in a garret. Is that something you've always been aware of?

MOR: Well, I *am* that solitary writer, actually, but, eventually, you have to come out of the garret in order to put what you've written on stage. And I mean, for a long time, I was scared and mistrustful of that part of the process, the handing over of the text, even up as far as when I wrote *Terminus*. You mentioned *Play* earlier. I wanted to stage *Terminus* in a similar way, because I was so bound up in its internal rhymes that I thought, 'if I give the actors any leeway at all with this they'll screw it up.' Stupid. So, I wanted to put them in a confining equivalent of Beckett's urns and have them perform the play in a kind of emotionless style that would, to the exclusion of everything else, obey the rules of rhyme and rhythm that the play, I felt, necessitated. But, a couple of weeks into rehearsal, I saw that it wasn't working. It was horrible – lifeless and stiff. And so, I dropped that method and allowed the actors to take the lead, only guiding them really, and discovered in the process what most good directors already know; the enormous value of the actors' contribution, their joy in text and command of character and, above all, their emotional imagination. This discovery occurred quite late, and so I had to change my approach incredibly quickly.

COB: It is interesting then, what you say, about this very fixed, controlled vision of how *Terminus* would work in terms of rhyme, rhythm, and movement, or lack of movement, and then to think about *Play*. Because Beckett had a very specific height for those urns, and the actors complained about the urns; that they could neither sit nor stand in them. Watching *Terminus*, what struck me was how uncomfortable the actors seemed to be, bodily ... but it worked. It added something to the play, that they looked so uncomfortable.

MOR: It's a good point. I suppose the freedom of performance I mentioned earlier was tempered by a very narrow area of movement. Jon Bauser's set was like a picture frame, or a mirror which had exploded inwards. There were these frozen shards of glass, and the actors stood on them, and they had to be slightly angled forward in a steep rake so we could see them. Initially, I thought, ok, we would have the actors standing throughout the play, and the first actor would speak for ten minutes, then the second, then the third, then the first again, and on like that (there were nine monologues of about ten minutes each). But in rehearsal I realized that, between monologues, each actor would have to stand completely still for twenty minutes waiting for their turn. So I had them sit down between monologues instead. And so, as uncomfortable as what you saw was, it could have been a lot worse. My actors were very patient. They understood the staging concept and so didn't complain.

We did *Terminus* here [at the Abbey in 2007]. Then we did it in Edinburgh, then Melbourne, and then we did a big tour of the U.S and Australia in 2011. I found it slightly frustrating that all the theatre managements who had booked us had, of course, booked in the *production*, so, even though the cast changed, each new actor giving a new interpretation (which was great), we couldn't change any of the production's other elements, and by that time I'd love to have completely reimagined the whole thing, just for a change, given it a different choreography, found some way to let the actors move about, go on and off stage. I mean, I loved the original version, and that focus was amazing, but we did it for a long time. I'd love to do a more open, more physically fluid version, at the very least so that the actors, when they're not speaking, can maybe go backstage and have a rest!

COB: Let me ask about Dublin as an influence in your work: the city-scape, the metropolis as its own character. For me, your plays are all about Dublin, but it's somewhere between a real city and a more surreal version of Dublin. In *Terminus* it's a nightmare city-scape. In *Howie and China* it's not-so-much the inner-city but the outlying bad-lands, suburbs that have become no-go areas. Or, is it even Dublin?

MOR: Yes. Or mostly. *Crestfall* is the only play that isn't specifically set there. For that, I wanted to create something that felt like a self-contained town, almost like a western, with two hotels, one pub, etc, but that wasn't specified as any one particular place. The version of *Crestfall* in the collected volume published by Nick Hern, is revised from the original, and I think it's a little bit clearer in that one.

But, yes, all the other plays are set in Dublin, and I agree with everything you've said. It's Dublin, but it's a heightened, slightly mythologized version. It's tough for me to even say what it is ...

COB: It's beyond articulation almost?

MOR: Not really. Probably just boringly complicated. *Terminus*, which is the most fantastical of them all, is also the most accurate geographically. You could follow the events on a map: the places the demon flies through, the road from Cashel to Dublin, the car chase at the end, etc.

Howie is sort of based in Tallaght, where I grew up, but none of the places the [characters] inhabit have real names; they're all invented. So, for example, there's the Mercy Loop, where the Howie surfs on top of the van, which was actually called the Fortunestown Lane. Or 'the New Shops', where the shops are built with their backs facing out; that's a mixture of a group of shops in Clondalkin and another group of shops in Tallaght. And so on.

Made in China, then, is more city-centre Dublin, but again, a more heightened, invented version.

COB: I want to talk now about narrative, and how you tell a story. I said earlier that you don't consciously try to fit in with a tradition of narrative Irish theatre. You don't see yourself as following on from a tradition of O'Casey or Yeats. However, in terms of globalization, contemporary capitalism, could it be that you're making a comment on Irish identity in terms of how Ireland is moving into a more globalized world? I'm thinking of the materialism of the jacket in *Made in China*, where a material thing that is so small can have such huge ramifications?

MOR: I've never consciously commented on anything in my stuff. I feel it simply isn't my job. Regarding Irishness, though, I can say this: growing up in 1970s Tallaght, we had no connection to Irish culture whatsoever. We had the English TV channels and we had books and movies and music from anywhere *but* Ireland, and so almost all of my earlier influences came from other countries.

And then, later, of course, I'm socializing with people who know all these Irish songs, and poems, all this Irish theatre, and I'm like, what the hell are they on about? Even now, there's a lot I haven't seen or read. Synge: I saw *Playboy of the Western World*. I didn't get it. A couple of O'Caseys. *Juno and the Paycock*. A love for these guys is something that probably should be in my DNA, but it isn't really.

COB: Well, that's a very interesting point, 'It should be in my DNA', because that's something I would argue against, that there is an 'Irish DNA'.

MOR: Exactly. And isn't it also a thing of, well, I'm looking at Friel, and I'm looking at Murphy, and I think they're both geniuses. I mean, Murphy! Just brilliant. A brilliant artist. An inspiration. But my love for both of these writers has nothing to do with the fact that they're Irish. It's to do with their skills as writers, their insights into humanity, their dramaturgy, their poetry. Their Irishness doesn't come into it. In fact, the focus on that would be a slight negative for me.

COB: So, now I want to talk about how you portray men, masculinity, and sexuality. Can we talk about 'hypermasculinity': the idea that these are really hard men, and that, say in something like *From Both Hips*, the good guys get punished rather than the bad guys. Maybe this is where people see correlations with Tarantino. But some people would argue that this is a very limiting and narrow version of masculinity; that there are, surely, many more ways of being a man than just this hard-man image. How would you answer the challenge that this could be, perhaps, a dangerous paradigm of manhood in the terms of social influence on young men?

MOR: I wouldn't. Those concerns are, I feel, outside of my responsibility, which is simply to write the best play I can. At the time, this maleness was simply the kind of thing I needed to explore. And, again, the Tarantino comparison is lazy. I would have actually been looking at Mamet, I was looking at *American Buffalo;* that's the territory I wanted to venture into. Less cartoony and more genuinely probing. And Pinter, particularly *The Homecoming*.

COB: The men in *The Homecoming* are very menacing, very scary.

MOR: Absolutely, very frightening.

COB: Is it because they're easier to write, those kind of men?

MOR: Not so much easier as more natural. I mean I don't do it much anymore. My last two plays, *Crestfall* and *Terminus*, they were mostly women, so I'm no longer as interested as I was in that sort of hard-man thing.

COB: Well, with the man in *Terminus* you did display a multi-layered character. He was full of all sorts of low self-esteem issues.

MOR: Well, yes, with him I was exploring the desire for fame and approval in the world. This was a man with incredibly low self-esteem, but also with a need to announce himself, to realize or to actualize himself through performance. Which is why, when he's hanging off the crane by his guts at the end, he says 'this will fuel me for an eternity in hell,' or whatever the line is – because that's feeding into this need that so many of us have, what we're seeing with shows like *The X-Factor*, everyone's desire to be famous. You can trace this on a very primal level back to ourselves as children, as babies, with this need to be taken care of, to feel like we're loved. I suppose most of our behaviour ties in with that.

COB: Well it's very interesting that you say it's all about performance, because one of the things I would say is that we perform our masculinity, that it's brought into being by doing, that it's not driven by this inner essence of manliness. And now you tell me that the man in *Terminus* was brought into being by what he did.

MOR: It's not just the performance. It's the performance *being witnessed*! It's not of any value unless it's witnessed. This guy, he was given an extraordinary singing voice by the devil, but when he tried to perform in front of people he couldn't, he was too shy. Which is not to say that when he was alone he couldn't do it. But what good is that? You need an audience. It's as if nothing any of us do is any good unless there's somebody there to see it, to witness it, or at least to hear about it. And I can say a little bit about my own psychology here. Growing up in Tallaght, it was a tough environment and a lot of the guys I was hanging around with were tough bastards, but I wasn't, and I think that was probably a pretty major source of insecurity for me. Or even shame. These were the guys I desperately wanted approval or acceptance from, but I was lacking in their eyes. I couldn't comfortably behave the way they did, and I suppose that left me (like so many writers) in the role more of observer than participant. Looking back, I was constantly frozen by thoughts of consequences, whereas these guys didn't think about stuff; they just *did* stuff, and it always seemed like it came completely naturally to them, and that there was something wrong with me for not being like them. I suppose, then, you get a bit older and discover there *are* people like you and you spend time with them and gradually become a little more comfortable with yourself.

When I began working in theatre, I was genuinely astonished by how thoughtful and compassionate most practitioners were, particularly actors, and there was an incredibly powerful sense of acceptance there which just blew me away.

But you don't think, 'do you know what, I'm going to write about these hard guys.' You just write and whatever comes out, comes out. But what was coming out was obviously something that had affected me.

COB: Was writing then a way of overcoming some trauma?

MOR: No, because it wasn't trauma.

COB: So just a general sense of misplacement, a sense of unease.

MOR: Yeah, maybe. But, also, bear in mind that most of those who influence you are exploring similar subjects. For example, I got hooked onto Mamet, not for his male subjects, but because of the sound of his dialogue. Simply that: the poetry. But then, Mamet was *also* writing about pretty tough bastards, so how much of the subject matter rubbed off on me too? I mean, men killing each other is the backbone of so much storytelling, right back to its beginning; you know, tales of war or revenge and whatever.

But then, I don't know. I often wonder how much of my impulse to write has been driven by a childish desire to show off, to be the bold boy, saying 'look how well I can describe someone getting their eyes popped out.' I mean you have these ideas about someone being hung up by their intestines, or someone else getting decimated under a truck – and that's the impulse. It's like a child saying, 'look what I can do, I can describe this horrible thing.'

But then you realize you've got to build a play around that, you've got to turn it into a proper story, and that's when you've got to start exploring more complex ideas for the thing to make any kind of narrative or psychological sense; and I find increasingly that that kind of exploration becomes the most satisfying part of the process.

COB: You've written three monologue plays now, and to some extent you've become associated with the form. Is your decision to use the monologue based on how that form can circumvent the logistics of representing acts of sex and violence onstage?

MOR: Not sex and violence, because they *can* be represented; but scale, pace, variety of location, fantastical elements which simply can't be created on stage except with language. And so, if I want to have a demon made out of worms flying around, I don't have to show it. I can just tell it. If you were to make a film of *Terminus* it would be difficult to bring to life. It would take a Hollywood size budget to render it convincingly. But, if you say, for example, 'there was a crowd of a million people,' we picture it. So, I suppose, in a way, it's about describing ...

COB: I think that's the key: that it's descriptive, that it's reporting ...

MOR: Yes. ... [O]r compelling the audience to create their own pictures. Actually, now that I think of it, you rarely, if ever, in fact, describe a *thing*, because that slows down your narrative too much. That was always a rule with me. If I say a car, I don't describe the car. I don't say 'a blue Nissan' because who cares? I say a car and you've got one in your head already.

COB: So, it's an awareness of what you are doing with the spectator always?

MOR: Yes, but once again, I can kind of see that now, but back then it was just something I did without being aware of it.

COB: We're back to the playwright's instinct we spoke of earlier then?

MOR: Absolutely. Someone once said that, particularly with *Terminus,* you'd always get a great visceral reaction in terms of the horror. You could see the audience covering their eyes. But from what? There was nothing to see. What's happening there is that the words are doing the work. The audience member has made the picture in their head already.

COB: And I think, perhaps, when you're telling these big, extreme stories, there is a sense that we need to move away from the narrative form of Irish drama because sometimes the story is too big, too extreme to be narrativized, so it needs to be reported.

MOR: Well, it's all narrative, really, but, yes, what you're saying is some stories are too big or too dense to be dramatized, so they need to be told in a form that's closer to traditional storytelling, maybe.

COB: What about building trust? Because the spectator has to trust the monologist?

MOR: Well, yes, that's essential. The drama in traditional theatre occurs between the characters on stage, the drama in the monologue play occurs between the performer and the audience, and so the audience needs to commit to being the second character, the listener. If they don't, it's not going to work. When we did *Crestfall* at the Gate, audiences generally didn't like it ...

COB: Perhaps the negative reactions were more to do with that space. The Gate – and that when people go to that space they expect certain things, which *Crestfall* was not?

MOR: Yeah, that might be true, but it's only part of the story. Part of the reason I rewrote it years later was that, in rereading it prior to its publication, I recognized certain dishonest impulses which I couldn't really get behind.

And this addresses the question of trust. Any artist has this issue of self-confidence which can be hugely beneficial or damaging, depending on how strong or weak it is at any given time. Mine was pretty low when I started that play, and I remember thinking: 'ok, this is going to be the coldest, darkest, most violent play I can come up with; it'll be devoid of humour or humanity and that's going to be the point of it.' But what that did was eliminate any potential connection, any trust, with the audience, and so the play was like an act of aggression towards them. And even though, despite this, the actors were able to access (or maybe manufacture) much of the humanity that was lacking, it was still sort of suffocating for the audience. I think, in my insecurity, it was like a defence mechanism of sorts, me saying, 'well, if you don't like it, that's fine – you're not supposed to.' Anyway: I really just closed off any points of identification or contact.

COB: Do you think that's maybe because it was your first play with an all-women cast?

MOR: No, that didn't make any difference to me. But it was the first time I'd ever said 'I'm going to do this definitive thing, I'm going to make this utterly cold and unforgiving.' And as such it was an experimental piece, I suppose. It feels a little unfair talking about it this way, because I thought the production was really strong and the actors' commitment to the piece, not to mention their courage, facing those kinds of audiences with that kind of material, was really awe-inspiring.

COB: I wonder how much of that led to *Terminus*, because that is a brutally honest play. There is such an honesty in those characters. Maybe it's about going back to move forward?

MOR: Absolutely, definitely. Those steps can be pretty painful at the time, but they have to be taken occasionally in order for an artist to grow. But when I look at *Terminus* now I just think, 'what were you thinking!?' Rhyme?

COB: So, why rhyme? That's where I see Milton coming through.

MOR: I rhymed a couple of lines by mistake, and then I said, maybe I'll try this as an experiment, write a few more like that, just to see where it goes. And suddenly, I'd done too much and gone too far to back down. At times it made the writing process so much tougher, but then there were days when it all flowed beautifully. I remember rehearsing the first production, thinking there was a big chance that the thing simply wouldn't work. But I was very happy with it.

COB: You directed the recent production of *Howie the Rookie* at the Project Arts Centre with Tom Vaughan-Lawlor. Is more directing on the cards?

MOR: Sure. I was in a very good place when I did *Howie*, because I'd directed before and I knew I could do it. But the original production was so brilliant. The actors [Karl Shiels and Aidan Kelly] were so amazing, and they were also so right, it was such perfect casting. Even now you couldn't find two people who were so right.

But when Anne Clarke from Landmark [Productions] came to me about a new *Howie* and asked, 'do you want to direct it?' I thought to myself, well, I could just do another version of what was done before, but, as far as I was concerned, the definitive version had already been done. And I thought, there has to be an approach here that'll really get me excited about returning to it. Then Tom [Vaughan-Lawlor] was mentioned, and I thought, Fuck! Yes, that guy's amazing. I'd seen him do *Arturo Ui* and *Saved* and I just thought he was incredible.

But then there was the question of who to pair him with. I couldn't think of anyone who could match him, and there really needs to be an equality of performance in those parts. You can't have an audience comparing the actors and finding one of them lacking.

So I thought maybe Tom could do both of them, and I remember being both excited and terrified by the idea. 'This can't work. Or can it?' I sensed there was something in the play about duality – the two characters being two aspects, maybe, of a particular type of man. You've got the Howie, who's a tough fucker. He fulfils all the criteria in terms of machismo, but is deeply lacking in self-confidence. The Rookie is the opposite of that. He is a ladies' man, completely confident, but lacking on a macho level. So in a sense they are two incomplete halves of a certain ideal of manhood. So I thought, 'Yeah, this might work.' We offered it to Tom and he said he'd do it, and I felt, all we can do now is fuck it up.'

He had the whole thing learnt before we went into rehearsal, which was great. We worked our arses off, all the same, and we just about got there. It was a very tough process, but a really rewarding one; very rigorous and very detailed and Tom loved it, and it all paid off at the end. I really thought it was an incredible performance.

On stage he wore pretty much what he wore in rehearsal; runners, jeans and a t-shirt, and the only concession we made toward differentiating the characters was to changing his t-shirt at the interval. Because it's not about an actor trying to convince us he's actually two different people; it's an actor creating two different people in front of us, and part of the show's power, I felt, came from our being completely honest about that.

COB: So, let's wrap it up – what's next? What projects are in the pipeline?

MOR: I've a new play for the Abbey which we're going to do for the Theatre Festival, 2014. It's a proper play, with characters who actually talk to each other! I can't really say what it's about, but I'll direct that too. I really enjoy the process now and I find it's far easier to take responsibility for the show myself, rather than giving it over to someone else. That way I don't have to worry constantly about someone else fucking it up – I'll be too busy doing that myself.

COB: Mark O'Rowe, thank you very much.

MOR: Thank you!

Performances and Bibliography

First Performances

The Aspidistra Code, presented as a rehearsed reading by National Association for Youth Drama, at the Peacock Theatre, 2nd December 1995.

Rundown, produced by Origin Theatre Company, at the International Bar, August 1996.

Anna's Ankle, produced by Bedrock Theatre, at Project @ the Mint, 17th February 1997.

From Both Hips, produced by Fishamble: The New Play Company, at Project Arts Centre, 27th June 1997.

Howie the Rookie, produced by the Bush Theatre, at the Bush Theatre, 10th February 1999.

Made in China, Produced by the Abbey Theatre, at the Peacock Theatre, 1st April 2001.

Crestfall, produced by Gate Theatre, at the Gate Theatre, 20th May 2003.

Terminus, produced by the Abbey Theatre, at the Peacock Theatre, 13th June 2007.

Our Few and Evil Days, produced by the Abbey Theatre, at the Abbey Theatre, 3rd October, 2014.

Films

Intermission, 2003. Brown Sauce Film Production, Brown Sauce Film Productions, Bord Scannan na hEireann, Company of Wolves, Irish Film Board (funding), Parallel Film Productions, Portman Film, UK Film Council. Written by Mark O'Rowe. Directed by John Carney.

Boy A, 2007. Cuba Pictures, Film Four. Screenplay by Mark O'Rowe after the novel *Boy A* by Jonathan Trigell. Directed by John Crowley.

Perrier's Bounty, 2009. Parallel Film Productions, Number 9 Films, Irish Film Board, Premiere Pictures. Written by Mark O'Rowe. Directed by Ian Fitzgibbon.

*Epithe*t, 2012. Young Vic Short Films. Written by Mark O'Rowe. Directed by Angus Jackson.

Broken, 2012. BBC Films, Bill Kenwright Films, Cuba Pictures, Lipsync Productions,Written by Mark O'Rowe after the novel *Broken* by Daniel Clay. Directed by Rufus Norris.

debris, 2013. Cuba Films, Parallel Pictures. Written and directed by Mark O'Rowe.

Published Plays and Screenplays

Mark O'Rowe, *Plays: One [The Aspidistra Code; From Both Hips; Made in China; Howie the Rookie; Crestfall]*. London: Nick Hern, 2011.

From Both Hips: Two Plays. London: Nick Hern, 1999.

Howie the Rookie. London: Nick Hern, 1999.

Made in China. London: Nick Hern, 2001.

Terminus. London: Nick Hern, 2011.

Our Few and Evil Days. London: Nick Hern, 2014.

Select Bibliography

Book Chapters

Middeke, Martin and Peter Paul Schnierer, eds. *The Methuen Drama Guide to Contemporary Irish Playwrights* (London: Methuen Drama, 2010), 345-364.

Walsh, Fintan, 'Impotent Masculinities in *Made in China* and *Intermission*.' In *Male Trouble: Masculinity and the Performance of Crisis* (Basingstoke: Palgrave Macmillan, 2010) 58-83.

Journal Articles

Fricker, Karen, 'Same Old Show: The Performance of Masculinity in Conor McPherson's *Port Authority* and Mark O'Rowe's *Made in China*', *The Irish Review* 29 (Autumn, 2002): 84-94.

Haughton, Miriam, 'Performing Power: Violence as Fantasy and Spectacle in Mark O'Rowe's *Made in China* and *Terminus*', *New Theatre Quarterly* 27, no. 2 (May 2011): 153-166.

Jordan, Eamonn, 'Project Mayhem: Mark O'Rowe's *Howie the Rookie*', *The Irish Review* 35 (Summer 2007): 117-131.

Lonergan, Patrick, 'I Do Repent and Yet I Do Despair: Beckettian and Faustian Allusions in Conor McPherson's *The Seafarer* and Mark O'Rowe's *Terminus*.' *ANQ: A Quarterly Journal of Short Articles, Notes and Reviews* 25, no. 1 (2012): 24-30.

Leeney, Cathy, 'Men in No-Man's Land: Performing Urban Liminal Spaces in Two Plays by Mark O'Rowe', *The Irish Review* 35 (Summer 2007): 108-116.

Biographies

Nelson Barre is a Hardiman Research Scholar and PhD candidate in Drama and Theatre Studies at the National University of Ireland, Galway. His research focuses largely on ritual, memory, and performance in contemporary Irish theatre and culture. His writing appears in *Comparative Drama* and *New Hibernia Review*, and he has forthcoming work on Enda Walsh.

Tim Barrett is a PhD candidate in the School of Drama, Film and Music at Trinity College, Dublin, working on the thesis "Monologue Drama in Ireland from 1964-2014: Form and Performativity" under the supervision of Professor Stephen Wilmer. He has presented research at the Irish Society for Theatre Research conference and at Trinity's School of Drama, Film and Music Research Seminar. He is a graduate of Birmingham University's MPhil in Playwriting Studies (2005) and holds an M.A. in Anglo-Irish Literature and Drama (1999) and a B.A. in Celtic Studies (1997) from University College Dublin.

David Clare is an IRC-funded postdoctoral research fellow based in the Moore Institute at the National University of Ireland, Galway. His journal articles have appeared (or will soon appear) in the *Irish Studies Review*, the *New Hibernia Review*, the *Irish University Review*, *Studies: An Irish Quarterly*, and *Emerging Perspectives*. Dr Clare has delivered numerous conference papers in Ireland, Britain, and North America on important figures from Irish drama, including George Farquhar, Oliver Goldsmith, R.B. Sheridan, Oscar Wilde, George Bernard Shaw, J.M. Synge, Lady Gregory, Samuel Beckett, Brendan Behan, Brian Friel, Marie Jones, Martin McDonagh, Mark O'Rowe, and Mark O'Halloran.

Thomas B. Costello is an Assistant Professor of Theatre and Speech at SUNY Dutchess, where he teaches Theatre History, Criticism, Acting, Directing, Shakespeare, and Speech. He is passionate about combining scholarly and pedagogical work in production; thus, his work as a producer, director, and scenographer has colored the stages of New York, London, Dublin, Prague, and beyond. He currently serves on the founding editorial board for the peer-reviewed *Stage Directors and Choreographers Society SDC Journal*, and other recent Irish theatre publications include a chapter in *The American as Foreigner on Stage: Portraits of the United States in International Drama* (2010).

Emma Creedon was awarded a PhD from University College Dublin in 2013. She has taught courses on English and Drama at UCD and at NUI Galway. Her monograph *Sam Shepard and the Aesthetics of Performance* will be published by Palgrave Macmillan in 2015. Her research has also been published in the peer-reviewed journals *Word and Text: A Journal of Literary Studies and Linguistics* and the *Journal of Contemporary Drama in English*. Her research interests include Modern American Drama, Surrealism, Modern and Contemporary Irish Drama and European Absurdism.

Jimmy Fay is Executive Producer of the Lyric Theatre, Belfast. He is a former Associate Artist of the Abbey Theatre, Artistic Director of Bedrock Productions and the original director and co-founder of the Dublin Fringe Festival. Among the productions he's directed are *Unidentified Human Remains and the True Nature of Love* by Brad Fraser (Bedrock), *Saved* by Edward Bond (Peacock), *The Resistible Rise of Arturo Ui* by Bertolt Brecht (Abbey), *Breaking Dad* by Paul Howard (Landmark) and *Pentecost* by Stewart Parker (Lyric).

Garry Hynes is a founding member and Director of Druid Theatre. In 1998 on Broadway, she became the first woman to receive a Tony Award for Direction for *The Beauty Queen of Leenane*. She is a recipient of many other Theatre Awards, including The Irish Times/ESB Irish Theatre Award for Best Director (2002) and a Special Tribute Award for her contribution to Irish Theatre in February 2005. She will direct the forthcoming production of Mark O'Rowe's adaptation of *Henry IV* later this year.

Sara Keating is a Cultural Journalist and Theatre Critic with *The Irish Times*. She received her PhD from the Samuel Beckett Centre at Trinity College Dublin in 2006, and has taught courses on Irish Theatre at Trinity College, Dublin, University College Dublin and New York University.

Aidan Kelly is from Ballybrack in County Dublin. He learned how to act doing youth theatre. After dropping out of art college he started acting for money. After many happy years working in Dublin and around the Ireland and beyond with The Abbey, Druid, Rough Magic and The Gate amongst others, he moved to London where he has worked with the National Theatre, The Royal Shakespeare Company, The Donmar Warehouse and in the West End. He also occasionally turns up on TV and in films.

Marie Kelly lectures in Drama and Theatre Studies at the School of Music and Theatre, University College Cork. She worked at the Abbey Theatre between 1993 and 2006, firstly as an Executive Assistant and subsequently as Casting Director. Marie has an MA in Modern Drama and Performance (2005) and a PhD in Drama Studies (2011), both from the School of English, Drama and Film at University College Dublin. Her book *The Theatre of Tom Mac Intyre: Strays from the Ether* was co-edited with Dr. Bernadette Sweeney (University of Montana) and published by Carysfort Press in 2010.

Cormac O'Brien has recently completed his PhD, entitled 'Acting the Man: Performing Masculinities in Contemporary Irish Theatre' at the School of English, Drama and Film at University College Dublin, where he teaches part-time. Working primarily in contemporary Irish and British theatre, Cormac researches queer theatre and queer histories, and gender and sexuality in performance. Cormac's newest project, 'Performance in the Age of AIDS' investigates how HIV and AIDS, and the bodies they occupy and the lives they affect, are represented in performance. Cormac has published several essays and book chapters in edited collections and journals such as *Irish University Review*, *Theatre Research International*, *Irish Theatre International*, and *The Hungarian Journal of English and American Studies*.

Harvey O'Brien teaches Film Studies at University College Dublin. He is the author of *Action Movies: The Cinema of Striking Back* (Columbia, 2012), *The Real Ireland: The Evolution of Ireland in*

Documentary Film (Manchester, 2004) and co-editor (with Ruth Barton) of *Keeping it Real: Irish Film and Television* (Wallflower, 2004). He is a member of the Board of Directors of the Irish Film Institute and a former Associate Director of the Boston Irish Film Festival. He has written articles for numerous publications and has written and spoken widely on film and theatre in popular print, online, at guest lectures in various public and academic institutions, and on radio.

Francis O'Connor is a stage designer and frequent collaborator with Garry Hynes. Awards Include Best Designer in the 1997 and 2000 The Irish Times/ESB Irish Theatre Awards.

Aisling O'Sullivan is an award-winning actress on stage and screen. She has worked regularly with Garry Hynes and Druid Theatre, and was nominated for The Irish Times Theatre Awards for her roles in *Big Maggie*, *Playboy of the Western World* and *Bailegangaire*, among others.

Emilie Pine lectures in modern drama at University College Dublin. She publishes in the field of Irish theatre, culture and memory studies and her monograph *The Politics of Irish Memory: Performing Remembrance in Contemporary Irish Culture* is published by Palgrave (2010). She is Director of the Irish Memory Studies Network and Assistant Editor of the *Irish University Review*.

Eileen Walsh is an award-winning stage and screen actress. She works regularly with Garry Hynes' Druid Theatre and originated the role of B in Terminus at the Abbey Theatre, for which she won an Irish Times Theatre Award for Best Actress.

Index

A

Abbey Theatre (Dublin), The, 1-2, 5, 15, 79, 89, 109, 137, 141, 155, 160-61
Afro-Celt Sound System, 21
Anderson, Ian-Lloyd, 137, 140
Andrews, Rachel, 60
Arditti, Paul, 59
Assembly Rooms (Edinburgh), The, 44
Aydon, Deborah, 42

B

Bausor, Jon, 92, 97
Beckett, Samuel, 8-9, 13, 22-23, 32, 43, 50, 58, 80, 143-45, 159, 161
  Catastrophe, 9
  Company, 13, 14, 18, 42, 65, 155, 161
  Molloy, 144
  Not I, 22
  Play, 92, 121, 143, 145, 155
  What Where?, 9
Bedrock Theatre Company, 8, 14, 65, 155, 160
Bernstein, Mashey, 81
Bond, Edward, 9, 131, 160
  Bingo, 131
Bradwell, Mike, 41-42
Brantley, Ben, 27-28, 32, 35, 39, 45
Brennan, Kate, 93, 103
Broadbent, Jim, 124
Bush Theatre, The, 3, 10, 28, 41, 155
Butler, Judith, 63, 74
Byrne, Gabriel, 123

C

Caldwell, Ellen M., 86, 88
Campbell, Joanne, 132
Carney, John, 14, 155
  Once, 14, 37, 65, 115, 117
Carney, Kieran, 14
Cartesian (see René Descartes), 4, 91, 98, 100-101
Cartwright, Jim, 58
Carty, Ciaran, 79, 88
Chekhov, Anton, 143
City Arts Centre (Dublin), The, 41
Civic Theatre (Dublin), The, 44
Clancy, Luke, 61
Coen Brothers, The, 23
Colgan, Michael, 49
Collins-Hughes, Laura, 95, 103, 106, 119
Conlon, Declan, 11, 132

Coulter, Colin, 15
Cronenberg, David, 98, 103
Crowley, John, 123, 127, 155
Cunningham, Liam, 126
Cusack, Sinéad, 137, 139

D

Damasio, Antonio, 95-96, 100-101, 103
Delaney, Padraic, 124
Demastes, William, 101, 103
Derrida, Jacques, 113, 119
Descartes, René, 97, 101, 103
Dickens, Charles, 143
Dostoyevsky, Fyodor, 143
Doyle, Roddy, 21
Druid Theatre Company, 79, 88, 161
Dublin Theatre Festival, The, 5
Dublin Youth Theatre (DYT), 8
Dunning, Nick, 11

E

Edwards, Aimee Ffion, 130
Ellroy, James, 143
Emms, Robert, 129

F

Farrell, Colin, 124
Fauconnier, Gilles, 96
Faulkner, William, 143
Fay, Jimmy, 1, 3, 7, 46, 89, 160
Featherstone, Mike, 111
Field, Syd, 123
Fiennes, Ralph, 108
Fishamble Theatre Company, 8, 18, 155
Fitzgibbon, Ian, 14, 156
Fricker, Karen, 83-84, 89, 157

Friel, Brian, 13, 21, 108, 143, 147, 159
Dancing at Lughnasa, 13
Faith Healer, 108, 143

G

Garage, 14
Garfield, Andrew, 127
Gate Theatre, The, 1, 49-51, 54, 71, 151, 155, 161
Gibbons, Fiachara, 39
Gladwell, Philip, 93, 103
Gleeson, Brendan, 124
Globe Theatre (London), The, 42, 103, 119
Gray, Roberta, 79
Grene, Nicholas, 108, 119

H

Hall, Tom, 14
Haughton, Miriam, 95
Hinds, Ciarán, 137, 139
Hynes, Garry, 1, 3, 50, 53, 58-59, 61, 88

I

Ignatiev, Noel, 22
In-Yer-Face Theatre, 106
Irvine, Andrea, 93, 103

J

Jordan, Eamonn, 1, 24, 69, 119, 125
Joyce, James, 36
Ulysses, 13

K

Kelly, Aidan, 1, 3, 10-11, 41, 93, 103, 152, 161

Keogan, Paul, 140
Kiberd, Declan, 21
Kinnear, Rory, 129

L

Laurence, Eloise, 129
Lee, Bruce, 22, 28, 125
Lee, Harper, 129
Leech, Patrick, 9
Leeney, Cathy, 132, 134, 157
Leonard, Elmore, 143
Lime, Harry, 123
Linehan, Niamh, 11
Lonergan, Patrick, 21, 64, 79-80, 108
Lunny, Dónal, 21
Lyons, Katie, 127

M

Mac Erlaine, Seán, 140
MacConghail, Fiach, 46
Macdonald, Kelly, 124
Mamet, David, 23, 38, 135, 142, 148-49
  American Buffalo, 148
Mangan, James Clarence, 22
Manganaro, Kevin, 36, 39
Marsh, Matthew, 130
McCabe, Richard, 131
McCarthy, Cormac, 143
McConachie, Bruce, 96, 103
McDonagh, Martin, 20, 28, 32, 119, 159
  Cripple of Inishmaan, The, 20
McElhatton, Michael, 14, 124
McKee, Robert, 123
McPherson, Conor, 52, 89, 108, 138, 143, 157
  Shining City, 138
  This Lime Tree Bower, 52
Meaney, Colm, 20, 124
Midler, Bette, 108, 117
Millard, Kathryn, 122, 135
Minetta Lane Theatre (Greenwich Village), The, 46
Miyoshi, Masao, 115
Moore, Thomas, 22
Mullan, Peter, 127
Mullen, Marie, 59, 61
Müller, Heiner, 9
  Obituary, 9
Murphy, Charlie, 137, 139
Murphy, Cillian, 124, 129
Murphy, Tom (actor), 11
Murphy, Tom (playwright), 113, 119
Murray, Rupert, 53, 59

N

Negra, Diane, 21
Nelmes, Jill, 122, 135
Norris, Rufus, 49, 127, 156

O

Ó Súilleabháin, Tomás, 126
O' Halloran, Mark
  Adam and Paul, 14
O'Brien, Eugene, 14
  Pure Mule, 14
O'Brien, John, 9
O'Connell, Dióg, 121, 135
O'Connor, Francis, 3, 51-52, 59, 61
O'Connor, Sinéad, 21
O'Rowe, Mark
  Aspidistra Code, The, 2, 8, 14-17, 22-23, 92, 143, 155-6
  Boy A, 121, 123-30, 133, 155
  Broken, 121, 127-29, 133, 156

Crestfall, 1-3, 49, 50-60, 63, 69, 71, 74-77, 132, 139, 146, 148, 151, 155-56
debris, 121, 130, 132-33
From Both Hips, 2, 8, 14-15, 18, 22-23, 139, 143, 148, 155-56
Howie the Rookie, 1, 3, 5, 10-12, 22, 27-41, 47, 53, 63, 66-68, 71, 74-75, 77, 80, 92, 102, 106, 125, 134, 138, 143, 144, 152, 155-57
Intermission, 2, 4, 14-20, 23, 121-28, 131, 155, 157
Made in China, 2, 4, 15, 19, 22-23, 79-89, 95, 103, 106, 147, 155-57
Our Few and Evil Days, 1-2, 4, 137-39, 155-56
Terminus, 1-4, 11, 50, 63, 66, 68, 71-74, 77, 91-107, 108, 109, 111, 113, 116, 118-19, 138, 143-57

O'Sullivan, Aisling, 1, 3, 51, 55, 59, 61, 132
O'Thomas, Mark, 122
Orwell, George, 16
  Keep the Aspidistra Flying, 7, 13, 16

P

Peacock Theatre, The (see Abbey Theatre, The), 3, 11, 79, 81, 92, 103, 155
Peckinpah, Sam, 11, 144
  Wild Bunch, The, 144
Pinter, Harold, 8, 23, 50, 80, 142-43, 148
  Homecoming, The, 148
Project Arts Centre (Dublin), The, 3, 5, 8, 14, 50, 152, 155

Q

Quinn, Bob, 21

R

Richardson, Brian, 3, 27, 32-36, 39
Richie, Guy, 141
Rothwell, Kenneth, 83, 89
Royal Shakespeare Company, The, 42, 161

S

Sackville Lounge (Dublin), The, 3, 41
Schwartz, Lynne, 32, 33, 39
Shakespeare, William, 10-11, 42, 54, 79, 81-89, 109, 131, 134, 141, 143, 160
  Henry IV Part 1, 3
Sheridan, Frances, 22
Shiels, Karl, 10-11, 42, 152
Singleton, Brian, 66, 77, 106, 119
Sopranos, The, 141
Steinberger, Rebecca, 81, 89
Stembridge, Gerard, 8, 15, 79, 81, 88-89, 103
Stewart, Patrick, 130
Stewart, Philip, 93, 103, 140
Synge, John Millington, 79, 147, 159

T

Tagore, Rabindranath, 22
Tallaght, Dublin suburb of, 3, 7, 14, 37, 44, 92, 141, 147, 149

Tarantino, Quentin, 38-39, 141, 148
Theatre of Cruelty, 3, 8-9, 65
Tolstoy, Leo, 143
Traub, Valerie, 82-84, 89
Tressell, Robert (née Noonan), 17
Trigell, Jonathan, 121, 155
Turner, Mark, 96

U

U2, 21

V

Van Sant, Gus
  My Own Private Idaho, 83, 89
Vaughan-Lawlor, Tom, 5, 137, 140, 152

W

Walker, Catherine, 132
Wallace, Clare, 102, 103
Walsh, Eileen, 1, 3, 53, 59, 61
Welles, Orson, 123
Whitaker, Jodie, 124
Williams, Tennessee, 80
Wills, Paul, 139, 140
Winn, Stephen, 30-31, 35, 40
Wiseman, Susan, 86, 89
Wycherley, Don, 124

Y

Yeats, William Butler, 22, 147
Young Vic Theatre, The, 131, 156

Z

Zinoman, Jason, 32, 40, 106, 119

Carysfort Press was formed in the summer of 1998. It receives annual funding from the Arts Council.

The directors believe that drama is playing an ever-increasing role in today's society and that enjoyment of the theatre, both professional and amateur, currently plays a central part in Irish culture.

The Press aims to produce high quality publications which, though written and/or edited by academics, will be made accessible to a general readership. The organisation would also like to provide a forum for critical thinking in the Arts in Ireland, again keeping the needs and interests of the general public in view.

The company publishes contemporary Irish writing for and about the theatre.

Editorial and publishing inquiries to:
Carysfort Press Ltd.,
58 Woodfield,
Scholarstown Road,
Rathfarnham,
Dublin 16,
Republic of Ireland.

T (353 1) 493 7383
E: info@carysfortpress.com
www.carysfortpress.com

HOW TO ORDER

TRADE ORDERS DIRECTLY TO:
Irish Book Distribution
Unit 12, North Park, North Road,
Finglas, Dublin 11.

T: (353 1) 8239580
E: mary@argosybooks.ie
www.argosybooks.ie

INDIVIDUAL ORDERS DIRECTLY TO:
eprint Ltd.
35 Coolmine Industrial Estate,
Blanchardstown, Dublin 15.
T: (353 1) 827 8860
E: books@eprint.ie
www.eprint.ie

FOR SALES IN NORTH AMERICA AND CANADA:
Dufour Editions Inc.,
124 Byers Road,
PO Box 7,
Chester Springs,
PA 19425,
USA

T: 1-610-458-5005
F: 1-610-458-7103

Radical Contemporary Theatre Practices by Women in Ireland

Edited by Miriam Haughton and Mária Kurdi

Radical Contemporary Theatre Practices by Women in Ireland is an important contribution to the fields of Irish theatre and performance studies, and gender and performance in Ireland. The essays and interviews explore the work of women directors, designers, and playwrights on both sides of the Irish Border, who are currently shaping theatre practice on the island. By gathering such an impressive range of material, Mária Kurdi and Miriam Haughton have produced a collection that offers a snapshot of radical practice on the Irish stage in the early 21st century.

ISBN 978-1-909325-75-3 €20 (Paperback)

The Theatre of Marie Jones: Telling Stories from the Ground up

Edited by Eugene McNulty and Tom Maguire

Marie Jones is one of the most prolific and popular writers working in Northern Irish theatre today. Her work has achieved local relevance and international recognition. From her earliest work with Charabanc in the early 1980s to the present day, Jones's work has engaged with Irish (and, more often than not, specifically Northern Irish) experience in ways that reveal the extent to which the personal is political in a distinctive form of popular theatre. This volume of essays engages critically with Jones's oeuvre, her reception in Ireland and beyond, and her position in the canon of contemporary drama.

ISBN 78-1-909325-65-4 €20 (Paperback)

Blue Raincoat Theatre Company

By Rhona Trench

Since its foundation in 1991, Blue Raincoat Theatre Company is Ireland's only full-time venue-based professional theatre ensemble and has become renowned for its movement, visual and aural proficiencies and precision. This book explores those signatures from a number of vantage points, conveying the complex challenges faced by Blue Raincoat as they respond to changing aesthetic and economic circumstances. Particular consideration is given to set, costume, sound and lighting design.

ISBN 78-1-909325-67-8 €20 (Paperback)

Across the Boundaries: Talking about Thomas Kilroy

Edited by: Guy Woodward

Thomas Kilroy's long and distinguished career is celebrated in this volume by new essays, panel discussions and an interview, reconsidering the work of one of Ireland's most intellectually ambitious and technically imaginative playwrights. Contributors are drawn from both the academic and theatrical spheres, and include Nicholas Grene, Wayne Jordan, Patrick Mason, Christopher Murray and Lynne Parker.

ISBN 78-1-909325-51-7 €15.00 (Paperback)

Tradition and Craft in Piano-Paying,
by Tilly Fleischmann

Edited by Ruth Fleischmann and John Buckley
DVD Musical examples: Gabriela Mayer

This is a document of considerable historical importance, offering an authoritative account of Liszt's teaching methods as imparted by two of his former students to whom he was particularly close. It contains much valuable information of a kind that is unavailable elsewhere. It records a direct and authentic oral tradition of continental European pianism going back to the nineteenth century.

ISBN 78-1-909325-524 €30 (Paperback)

Wexfour: John Banville, Eoin Colfer, Billy Roche, Colm Toibin

Edited by Ben Barnes
A dedication of four short plays by Wexford writers to celebrate the 40th Anniversary of Wexford Arts Centre.

ISBN 78-1-909325-548 €10

For the Sake of Sanity: Doing things with humour in Irish performance

Edited by Eric Weitz

Humour claims no ideological affiliation – its workings merit inspection in any and every individual case, in light of the who, what, where and when of a joke, including the manner of performance, the socio-cultural context, the dynamic amongst participants, and who knows how many other factors particular to the instance. There as many insights to be gained from the deployment of humour in performance as people to think about it – so herein lie a healthy handful of responses from a variety of perspectives.

For the Sake of Sanity: *Doing things with humour in Irish performance* assembles a range of essays from practitioners, academics, and journalists, all of whom address the attempt to make an audience laugh in various Irish contexts over the past century. With a general emphasis on theatre, the collection also includes essays on film, television and stand-up comedy for those insights into practice, society and culture revealed uniquely through instances of humour in performance.

ISBN 78-1-909-325-56-2 €20

Stanislavski in Ireland: Focus at Fifty

Edited by Brian McAvera and Steven Dedalus Burch

Stanislavski in Ireland: Focus at Fifty is an insight into Ireland's only arthouse theatre from the people who were there. Through interviews, articles, short memoirs and photographs, the book tracks the theatre from its inception, detailing the period under its founder Deirdre O'Connell and then the period following Joe Devlin's arrival as its new artistic director. Many of Ireland's leading theatre and film artists trained and worked at Focus, including Gabriel Byrne, Joan Bergin, Olwen Fouèrè, Brendan Coyle, Rebecca Schull, Johnny Murphy, Sean Campion, Tom Hickey and Mary Elizabeth and Declan Burke-Kennedy. The book comes complete with a chronological list of productions.

ISBN 78-1-909325-43-2 €20

Breaking Boundaries. An Anthology of Original Plays from the Focus Theatre

Edited by Steven Dedalus Burch

Almost from the beginning, since 1970, new plays became part of the Focus's repertory.
Of the seven plays in this anthology, all exhibit a range in styles from Lewis Carroll's fantastical world (*Alice in Wonderland* by Mary Elizabeth Burke-Kennedy), to a couple on the brink of a philandering weekend disaster (*The Day of the Mayfly* by Declan Burke-Kennedy), to a one-man show about Jonathan Swift (*Talking Through His Hat* by Michael Harding), an examination of two shoplifting thieves and the would-be writer who gets in their way (*Pinching For My Soul* by Elizabeth Moynihan), a battle royal between two sides of a world-famous painter (*Francis and Frances* by Brian McAvera), the reactions of multiple New Yorkers to that moment in September, 2011 (*New York Monologues* by Mike Poblete), to the final days of an iconic movie star (*Hollywood Valhalla* by Aidan Harney).

ISBN 78-1-909325-42-5 €20

The Art Of Billy Roche: Wexford As The World

Edited by Kevin Kerrane

Billy Roche – musician, actor, novelist, dramatist, screenwriter – is one of Ireland's most versatile talents. This anthology, the first comprehensive survey of Roche's work, focuses on his portrayal of one Irish town as a microcosm of human life itself, elemental and timeless. Among the contributors are fellow artists (Colm Tóibín, Conor McPherson, Belinda McKeon), theatre professionals (Benedict Nightingale, Dominic Dromgoole, Ingrid Craigie), and scholars on both sides of the Atlantic.

ISBN 78-1-904505-60-0 €20

The Theatre of Conor McPherson: 'Right beside the Beyond'

Edited by Lilian Chambers and Eamonn Jordan

Multiple productions and the international successes of plays like *The Weir* have led to Conor McPherson being regarded by many as one of the finest writers of his generation. McPherson has also been hugely prolific as a theatre director, as a screenwriter and film director, garnering many awards in these different roles. In this collection of essays, commentators from around the world address the substantial range of McPherson's output to date in theatre and film, a body of work written primarily during and in the aftermath of Ireland's Celtic Tiger period. These critics approach the work in challenging and dynamic ways, considering the crucial issues of morality, the rupturing of the real, storytelling, and the significance of space, violence and gender. Explicit considerations are given to comedy and humour, and to theatrical form, especially that of the monologue and to the ways that the otherworldly, the unconscious and supernatural are accommodated dramaturgically, with frequent emphasis placed on the specific aspects of performance in both theatre and film.

ISBN 78 1 904505 61 7 €20

The Story of Barabbas, The Company

Carmen Szabo

Acclaimed by audiences and critics alike for their highly innovative, adventurous and entertaining theatre, Barabbas The Company have created playful, intelligent and dynamic productions for over 17 years. Breaking the mould of Irish theatrical tradition and moving away from a text dominated theatre, Barabbas The Company's productions have established an instantly recognizable performance style influenced by the theatre of clown, circus, mime, puppetry, object manipulation and commedia dell'arte. This is the story of a unique company within the framework of Irish theatre, discussing the influences that shape their performances and establish their position within the history and development of contemporary Irish theatre. This book addresses the overwhelming necessity to reconsider Irish theatre history and to explore, in a language accessible to a wide range of readers, the issues of physicality and movement based theatre in Ireland.

ISBN 78-1-904505-59-4 €25

Irish Drama: Local and Global Perspectives

Edited by Nicholas Grene and Patrick Lonergan

Since the late 1970s there has been a marked internationalization of Irish drama, with individual plays, playwrights, and theatrical companies establishing newly global reputations. This book reflects upon these developments, drawing together leading scholars and playwrights to consider the consequences that arise when Irish theatre travels abroad.

Contributors: Chris Morash, Martine Pelletier, José Lanters, Richard Cave, James Moran, Werner Huber, Rhona Trench, Christopher Murray, Ursula Rani Sarma, Jesse Weaver, Enda Walsh, Elizabeth Kuti

ISBN 78-1-904505-63-1 €20

What Shakespeare Stole From Rome

Edited by Brian Arkins

What Shakespeare Stole From Rome analyses the multiple ways Shakespeare used material from Roman history and Latin poetry in his plays and poems. From the history of the Roman Republic to the tragedies of Seneca; from the Comedies of Platus to Ovid's poetry; this enlightening book examines the important influence of Rome and Greece on Shakespeare's work.

ISBN 78-1-904505-58-7 €20

Polite Forms

Harry White

Polite Forms is a sequence of poems that meditates on family life, remembering and reimagining scenes from childhood and adolescence through the formal composure of the sonnet, so that the uniformity of this framing device promotes a tension. Throughout the collection there is a constant preoccupation with the difference between actual remembrance and the illumination or meaning which poetry can afford. Some of the poems 'rewind the tapes of childhood' across two or three generations, and all of them are akin to pictures at an exhibition which survey individual impressions of childhood and parenthood in a thematically continuous series of portraits drawn from life. This is his first collection of poetry.

Harry White is Professor of Music at University College Dublin.

ISBN 78-1-904505-55-6 €10

Ibsen and Chekhov on the Irish Stage

Edited by Ros Dixon and Irina Ruppo Malone

Ibsen and Chekhov on the Irish Stage presents articles on the theories of translation and adaptation, new insights on the work of Brian Friel, Frank McGuinness, Thomas Kilroy, and Tom Murphy, historical analyses of theatrical productions during the Irish Revival, interviews with contemporary theatre directors, and a round-table discussion with the playwrights, Michael West and Thomas Kilroy.

Ibsen and Chekhov on the Irish Stage challenges the notion that a country's dramatic tradition develops in cultural isolation. It uncovers connections between past productions of plays by Ibsen and Chekhov and contemporary literary adaptations of their works by Irish playwrights, demonstrating the significance of international influence for the formation of national canon.

ISBN 78-1-904505-57-0 €20

Tom Swift Selected Plays

With an introduction by Peter Crawley.

The inaugural production of Performance Corporation in 2002 matched Voltaire's withering assault against the doctrine of optimism with a playful aesthetic and endlessly inventive stagecraft.

Each play in this collection was originally staged by the Performance Corporation and though Swift has explored different avenues ever since, such playfulness is a constant. The writing is precise, but leaves room for the discoveries of rehearsals, the flesh of the theatre. All plays are blueprints for performance, but several of these scripts – many of which are site-specific and all of them slyly topical – are documents for something unrepeatable.

ISBN 78-1-904505-56-3 €20

Synge and His Influences: Centenary Essays from the Synge Summer School

Edited by Patrick Lonergan

The year 2009 was the centenary of the death of John Millington Synge, one of the world's great dramatists. To mark the occasion, this book gathers essays by leading scholars of Irish drama, aiming to explore the writers and movements that shaped Synge, and to consider his enduring legacies. Essays discuss Synge's work in its Irish, European and world contexts – showing his engagement not just with the Irish literary revival but with European politics and culture too. The book also explores Synge's influence on later writers: Irish dramatists such as Brian Friel, Tom Murphy and Marina Carr, as well as international writers like Mustapha Matura and Erisa Kironde. It also considers Synge's place in Ireland today, revealing how *The Playboy of the Western World* has helped to shape Ireland's responses to globalisation and multiculturalism, in celebrated productions by the Abbey Theatre, Druid Theatre, and Pan Pan Theatre Company.

Contributors include Ann Saddlemyer, Ben Levitas, Mary Burke, Paige Reynolds, Eilís Ní Dhuibhne, Mark Phelan, Shaun Richards, Ondřej Pilný, Richard Pine, Alexandra Poulain, Emilie Pine, Melissa Sihra, Sara Keating, Bisi Adigun, Adrian Frazier and Anthony Roche.

ISBN 78-1-904505-50-1 €20.00

Constellations - The Life and Music of John Buckley

Benjamin Dwyer

Benjamin Dwyer provides a long overdue assessment of one of Ireland's most prolific composers of the last decades. He looks at John Buckley's music in the context of his biography and Irish cultural life. This is no hagiography but a critical assessment of Buckley's work, his roots and aesthetics. While looking closely at several of Buckley's compositions, the book is written in a comprehensible style that makes it easily accessible to anybody interested in Irish musical and cultural history.   *Wolfgang Marx*

As well as providing a very readable and comprehensive study of the life and music of John Buckley, Constellations also offers an up-to-date and informative catalogue of compositions, a complete discography, translations of set texts and the full libretto of his chamber opera, making this book an essential guide for both students and professional scholars alike.

ISBN 78-1-904505-52-5 €20.00

'Because We Are Poor': Irish Theatre in the 1990s

Victor Merriman

"Victor Merriman's work on Irish theatre is in the vanguard of a whole new paradigm in Irish theatre scholarship, one that is not content to contemplate monuments of past or present achievement, but for which the theatre is a lens that makes visible the hidden malaises in Irish society. That he has been able to do so by focusing on a period when so much else in Irish culture conspired to hide those problems is only testimony to the considerable power of his critical scrutiny." Chris Morash, NUI Maynooth.

ISBN 78-1-904505-51-8 €20.00

Buffoonery and Easy Sentiment':
Popular Irish Plays in the Decade Prior to the Opening of The Abbey Theatre

Christopher Fitz-Simon

In this fascinating reappraisal of the non-literary drama of the late 19th - early 20th century, Christopher Fitz-Simon discloses a unique world of plays, players and producers in metropolitan theatres in Ireland and other countries where Ireland was viewed as a source of extraordinary topics at once contemporary and comfortably remote: revolution, eviction, famine, agrarian agitation, political assassination.

The form was the fashionable one of melodrama, yet Irish melodrama was of a particular kind replete with hidden messages, and the language was far more allusive, colourful and entertaining than that of its English equivalent.

ISBN 78-1-9045505-49-5 €20.00

The Theatre of Tom Mac Intyre: 'Strays from the ether'

Eds. Bernadette Sweeney and Marie Kelly

This long overdue anthology captures the soul of Mac Intyre's dramatic canon – its ethereal qualities, its extraordinary diversity, its emphasis on the poetic and on performance – in an extensive range of visual, journalistic and scholarly contributions from writers, theatre practitioners.

ISBN 78-1-904505-46-4 €25

Irish Appropriation Of Greek Tragedy

Brian Arkins

This book presents an analysis of more than 30 plays written by Irish dramatists and poets that are based on the tragedies of Sophocles, Euripides and Aeschylus. These plays proceed from the time of Yeats and Synge through MacNeice and the Longfords on to many of today's leading writers.

ISBN 78-1-904505-47-1 €20

Alive in Time: The Enduring Drama of Tom Murphy

Ed. Christopher Murray

Almost 50 years after he first hit the headlines as Ireland's most challenging playwright, the 'angry young man' of those times Tom Murphy still commands his place at the pinnacle of Irish theatre. Here 17 new essays by prominent critics and academics, with an introduction by Christopher Murray, survey Murphy's dramatic oeuvre in a concerted attempt to define his greatness and enduring appeal, making this book a significant study of a unique genius.

ISBN 78-1-904505-45-7 €25

Performing Violence in Contemporary Ireland

Edited by Lisa Fitzpatrick

This interdisciplinary collection of fifteen new essays by scholars of theatre, Irish studies, music, design and politics explores aspects of the performance of violence in contemporary Ireland. With chapters on the work of playwrights Martin McDonagh, Martin Lynch, Conor McPherson and Gary Mitchell, on Republican commemorations and the 90th anniversary ceremonies for the Battle of the Somme and the Easter Rising, this book aims to contribute to the ongoing international debate on the performance of violence in contemporary societies.

ISBN 78-1-904505-44-0 €20

Deviant Acts: Essays on Queer Performance

Ed. David Cregan

This book contains an exciting collection of essays focusing on a variety of alternative performances happening in contemporary Ireland. While it highlights the particular representations of gay and lesbian identity it also brings to light how diversity has always been a part of Irish culture and is, in fact, shaping what it means to be Irish today.

ISBN 978-1-904505-42-6 €20

Plays and Controversies: Abbey Theatre Diaries 2000-2005

Ben Barnes

In diaries covering the period of his artistic directorship of the Abbey, Ben Barnes offers a frank, honest, and probing account of a much commented upon and controversial period in the history of the national theatre. These diaries also provide fascinating personal insights into the day-to-day pressures, joys, and frustrations of running one of Ireland's most iconic institutions.

ISBN 78-1-904505-38-9 €25

Interactions: Dublin Theatre Festival 1957-2007. Irish Theatrical Diaspora Series: 3

Eds. Nicholas Grene and Patrick Lonergan with Lilian Chambers

For over 50 years the Dublin Theatre Festival has been one of Ireland's most important cultural events, bringing countless new Irish plays to the world stage, while introducing Irish audiences to the most important international theatre companies and artists. Interactions explores and celebrates the achievements of the renowned Festival since 1957 and includes specially commissioned memoirs from past organizers, offering a unique perspective on the controversies and successes that have marked the event's history. An especially valuable feature of the volume, also, is a complete listing of the shows that have appeared at the Festival from 1957 to 2008.

ISBN 78-1-904505-36-5 €20

Synge: A Celebration

Edited by Colm Tóibín

A collection of essays by some of Ireland's most creative writers on the work of John Millington Synge, featuring Sebastian Barry, Marina Carr, Anthony Cronin, Roddy Doyle, Anne Enright, Hugo Hamilton, Joseph O'Connor, Mary O'Malley, Fintan O'Toole, Colm Toibin, Vincent Woods.

ISBN 978-1-904505-14-3 €15

www.ingramcontent.com/pod-product-compliance
Lightning Source LLC
Chambersburg PA
CBHW052051220426
43663CB00012B/2527